Thinking Spiritually in Small Groups

Thinking Spiritually in Small Groups

The Practice of Mystical Reflection

by
DANN WIGNER

CASCADE *Books* • Eugene, Oregon

THINKING SPIRITUALLY IN SMALL GROUPS
The Practice of Mystical Reflection

Copyright © 2022 Dann Wigner. All rights reserved. Except for brief quotations in critical publications or reviews, no part of this book may be reproduced in any manner without prior written permission from the publisher. Write: Permissions, Wipf and Stock Publishers, 199 W. 8th Ave., Suite 3, Eugene, OR 97401.

Cascade Books
An Imprint of Wipf and Stock Publishers
199 W. 8th Ave., Suite 3
Eugene, OR 97401

www.wipfandstock.com

PAPERBACK ISBN: 978-1-6667-0835-6
HARDCOVER ISBN: 978-1-6667-0836-3
EBOOK ISBN: 978-1-6667-0837-0

Cataloguing-in-Publication data:

Names: Wigner, Dann, author.

Title: Thinking spiritually in small groups : the practice of mystical reflection / Dann Wigner.

Description: Eugene, OR: Cascade Books, 2022 | Includes bibliographical references.

Identifiers: ISBN 978-1-6667-0835-6 (paperback) | ISBN 978-1-6667-0836-3 (hardcover) | ISBN 978-1-6667-0837-0 (ebook)

Subjects: LCSH: Mysticism—Christianity. | Spiritual formation. | Church group work.

Classification: BV5082.3 .W545 2022 (paperback) | BV5082.3 (ebook)

04/25/22

Unless otherwise specified, biblical quotations are from *The Book of Common Prayer and Administration of the Sacraments and Other Rites and Ceremonies of the Church: Together with the Psalter or Psalms of David; According to the Use of the Episcopal Church*, copyright @ 1979, 2007, Church Publishing. Used by permission. All rights reserved.

Scripture quotations from the New Revised Standard Version of the Bible, copyright @ 1989, Division of Christian Education of the National Council of Churches of Christ in the USA are used by permission. All rights reserved.

Scripture quotations from *The Message*, copyright @ 1993, 1994, 1995, 1996, 2000, 2001, 2002, 2005, are used by permission of NavPress Publishing Group.

Contents

Preface | vii
Acknowledgments | ix

CHAPTER 1
Introduction | 1

CHAPTER 2
What Is a Mystical Experience? | 8

CHAPTER 3
***Lectio Divina* and Centering Prayer** | 22

CHAPTER 4
The Method of Mystical Reflection | 31

CHAPTER 5
Group Dynamics | 50

CHAPTER 6
Examples of Mystical Experiences | 74

Bibliography | 111
Index | 115

Preface

Let me start with a confession: I love method books. I love learning new skills, and I think in step-by-step terms. However, one of my pet peeves is reading a book in which the author waits and waits and waits to tell you the method until the very end. In this light, I want to give you the basic method of mystical reflection—just the bullet points—so you can see it from the beginning. In the following chapters, I will go into great detail about my reasons for developing the method and what each step entails, but let's just get started with the step-by-step here:

1. Settling into the Space
2. Prayer for Guidance
3. First Reading/Telling of a Mystical Experience (ME)
4. First Centering Prayer Period
5. Second Reading/Telling of an ME
6. Second Centering Prayer Period
7. Sharing Time
8. Ending Prayer for Guidance and Parting

Those are the steps for the group meeting. We'll jump into these pieces as we go, but if you want to see them up front, then here they are. Eight steps to integrating mystical experiences into your spirituality and the spirituality of your community. Now let's start exploring them together.

Acknowledgments

According to the old proverb, "It takes a village to raise a child." I think that saying is also true for most books and especially true for a book that describes a new method. Methods are not developed in a vacuum. Even the best theoretical method fails if it doesn't work for people in practice. In light of this framework, I have a lot of people to thank for the book you see before you.

First, some of the people who have contributed to this book I don't even know on a first-name basis. In fact, they may not even know that they have contributed. I'm speaking of those who have visited my website (http://spiritualitystepbystep.com/) or my YouTube channel (https://www.youtube.com/channel/UCJq5DInx-CKW5Ld_Qv4iRRNQ). Along with those who have purchased my previous book, this group has demonstrated to me that there is interest in making spirituality simpler, demystified mysticism, so to speak. They have also shown me that what I have to say does help others to start in the various areas of spirituality—spiritual practices, mystical experiences, and mystical theology. So, thank you! This method and book wouldn't be here without you. Never be afraid to just begin in spirituality, and I hope you find this new tool useful to do just that.

Next, there are some people who have contributed to the publication process invaluably—those who have taken the time to review the manuscript, provide constructive editorial comments, or endorsements for publication. Especially, thank you to Cascade Books and Rodney Clapp, my editor, for all of your hard work!

Acknowledgments

Third, I have to say thank you to a very special group of people—those who participated in my first mystical reflection groups. Your feedback, comments, and willingness to experiment are the real reason that this method is anything more than an interesting idea at the back of my mind. Specifically, thank you so much to Rev. Brandon Hudson, Rev. David Bauman, Kelsey Leftwich-Yazell, Susan Sanders, Rev. John and Barbara Simpson, Rev. Cameron Spoor, Rev. Kevin-Antonio Smallwood, and Rev. Dr. Caroline Carson. Thank you! Thank you! Thank you! We had so much fun together.

Last, and most importantly, I have to thank my wonderful wife, the Rev. Leann Wigner. I think that people participated in these mystical reflection groups for your cooking far more than any method that I could dream up. However, your contribution goes so much deeper than that. Your eagerness and support in participating in mystical reflection, offering insightful advice on how to increase the relational aspects of the method, willingness to share your own experiences, and your editorial help as the manuscript took form were essential. In a real way, this book is as much yours as it is mine. "Thank you" is not enough to say; I can't imagine how you've put up with me these past seventeen years. I love you.

Chapter 1

Introduction

Mystical experiences are happening every day, yet—as amazing as the experiences can be—it is often difficult to integrate these experiences into the rest of our lives. As a result, I have developed a simple small group method, which I call *mystical reflection*, which blends centering prayer and *lectio Divina* in order to give some structure to the personal and communal integration of mystical experiences. Mystical reflection is a simple method for participating in a mystical experience so that we can step into a living, breathing engagement with the world to see the deeper meaning in our everyday lives. My aim in this book is to provide a small group method, but the context of mystical experiences themselves is quite complex. As a result, I would like to unpack my thought process for you in the rest of this introduction through a story, a reason, and an idea.

A Story

One day I had a very memorable meeting that occurred as part of the research for my dissertation. I was interviewing people at various churches concerning spiritual borrowing, which is the activity of borrowing a spiritual practice from one tradition and utilizing/

reinterpreting it in another tradition.[1] Along the way, I had a fascinating conversation with an individual who had recently had a profound mystical experience: *the baptism of the Holy Spirit*. While he was politely interested in talking about the practices which I was researching, his true eagerness gushed out of his experience. As a result, our lengthy conversation ranged all over the map, but I was quite struck by one question in particular which he asked me. He asked me why these types of profound religious experiences had stopped, why people no longer experienced God directly: "What was it that caused us to stop being filled with the Holy Spirit and actually moving in this world?" While this was only one question in a much larger conversation, it worried me, and my answer worried my interview participant in turn. I responded: "It didn't stop. We just stopped looking for it."

This exchange is a microcosm of what I've said and seen in hundreds of less formal conversations. Often, people have talked to me about a mystical experience they have had, or a person will express a desire to have mystical experiences, but they believe that such experiences are only for a select few, they are historical anomalies, or they are somewhat suspect for one reason or another. Such a persistence of this mentality of scarcity concerning mystical experiences was the first glimmer for me of the need for a method of mystical reflection. Mystical experiences occur far more often than most people think, as often as one out of every five persons[2] or, perhaps, even as commonly as one out of two.[3] My personal story above showed me a bit of a disconnection between common understandings of the term *mystical experience* (or, specifically, *baptism of the Holy Spirit* in that case) and our own common everyday experience. In other words, many think that mystical experiences are something that used to happen more often, but they are infrequent now.

Honestly, my subsequent experiences in talking to people about mysticism and mystical practices have demonstrated two

1. Wigner, *Sociology of Mystic Practices*, 1–4.
2. Paper, *Mystic Experience*, 61, 138.
3. Heimlich, "Mystical Experiences," lines 1–2.

Introduction

unique camps of people that group around this misunderstanding. The first group, which is typically a bit smaller, consists of people who have had mystical experiences, but they feel inhibited—or perhaps even ashamed—to talk about them. They often feel that people will think that they are crazy or at least weird. These "experience-ers" don't feel like anyone else has had an experience like their own. The second group, which is typically larger, but not as much as one might think, consists of people who do not have mystical experiences, or at least they are not having mystical experiences so fantastic that they label them in that way. These persons are asking questions much like the person in my story—why doesn't the spiritual realm break into our world anymore? What's wrong? Why is God silent? That interview encounter started me looking at the common misunderstandings concerning the frequency of mystical experiences, but it has taken the intervening years for me to work out the reason why these issues bother me so intensely.

A Reason

My reason for being upset is best expressed in terms of a belief and an accompanying principle. The disconnection between those who have mystical experiences and those who don't bothers me so much because of a theological belief that is central for me: God speaks. Following closely on the heels of that belief, for me, is a principle. The foundational theological principle at stake in mystical reflection is that if one person has an experience of God, then all can grow from it. Mystical experiences need to be shared for different reasons that coalesce around the two groups I mentioned earlier. For many of us who do not have mystical experiences, or who do not have mystical experiences of the obvious or fantastic variety, we need to have tangible, personal contact with these experiences. We need to see and hear that these experiences are real, that extraordinary contact with God is not only possible as a theoretical posit or historical anecdote, but also that our neighbors, friends, and family have encountered God in this way. It makes

God, the Spiritual, and the Infinite more immediate and more real to us. As such, it is invaluable for these mystical experiences to be shared with us. Incidentally, that's also why I advocate this method for *group* sharing.

Why share mystical experiences in a group? There are many avenues to share and savor mystical experiences with a spiritual director, clergyperson, or therapist on an individual basis. That pathway can be of immeasurable help to the experiencer in *interpreting* his/her own experiences. **I do not advocate that these mystical reflection groups try to interpret the mystical experience for the one who experienced it;** rather, it is about how new experiences of shared relationship can deepen members of the group spiritually through hearing the story of that mystical experience. This group method is not at odds with interpretation of mystical experience in one-to-one spiritual direction; rather, it is a supplementary method. The two types of relational interaction (one-to-one and group) have different purposes in looking at the same experience. On the one hand, the spiritual direction relationship builds spirituality on the individual level, and, on the other hand, a mystical reflection group builds spirituality on the communal level. Both are necessary for a full and multitextured spirituality. A last point here is the possibility that group mystical reflection, which does not require the presence of a spiritual director, may also help the individual who has had a mystical experience when a one-to-one spiritual direction relationship is not possible. After all, there are many places where spiritual directors are in short supply.

It is vital that mystical experiences do not remain unshared and uninterpreted completely, for these experiences are so powerful, yet so dissimilar from other types of experience, that people need support in interpreting and integrating them into their lives. Mystical experience by its very definition is an out-of-the-ordinary type of experience, though often in a subtle way. It speaks more loudly than everyday experience; it cries out to be noticed. Without some type of outlet for this type of experience, whether individually or corporately, the experience sits there in a person's psyche with nowhere to go. If this happens, then it is all too easy for a person to just disregard the experience, interpret it entirely idiosyncratically, or explain it away as a meaningless coincidence.[4] On the other hand, it is equally tempting to begin to think that her/his mystical experience is the only type of experience in life that counts.[5] Everything else in life is gray in comparison to that bright, shining moment lost in nostalgic memory.[6] The reason for this method of mystical reflection is to have an option for what to do with a mystical experience other than lock it away in the labyrinthine corridors of our minds, unable to be shared with another living human being as more than a charming anecdote. It is this reason, as much as the foregoing story, that led me to conclude that there needs to be a way to discuss mystical experiences with each other in such a way that every person's spirituality may be enriched and deepened through that sharing—and to be able to do so in a group rather than only in one-on-one spiritual direction.

An Idea

Simply stated, my idea is to provide a method to aid people to share their mystical experiences in groups. I'm an ardent advocate of methodical approaches. As is evident in my previous book, *Just Begin: A Sourcebook of Spiritual Practices*, I'm passionate about providing simple, easy-to-understand methods for exploring mystical *practices*. An easy entry point for dealing with mystical *experiences* is needed to complement entry points into mystical practices. As a little bit of terminological delineation, mystical *practices* are the spiritual habits, routines, and disciplines that we all can set out to do with active intentions such as prayer, *lectio Divina*, the Rosary, and so forth. Mystical *experiences*, on the other hand, are the relatively more passive moments which happen to a person that fall outside the typical flow of everyday experience and can only be described as encounters with the Spirit, the Infinite,

---

4. Alston, "Mysticism and the Perpetual Awareness of God," 205.
5. Mavrodes, "Real v. Deceptive," 237–38.
6. Huxley, *Perennial Philosophy*, 68.

or God. Consequently, I had the idea that a group of interested, committed—though by no means expert—people could fruitfully listen to the story of a mystical experience; that they could receive that story in a prayerful, meditative, and safe space; and that they could build their own spirituality *directly* through encountering mystical experiences as a group. Accordingly, I began drafting possible methods and asking friends and acquaintances to participate in some pilot groups. I think that the results give us a place to begin exploring mystical experiences together. Discussing these experiences in a group helped my two distinct categories noted above—the mystical experiencers and those who thought mystical experiences had ceased—meet and realize that neither are mystical experiences so rare, nor are those who have them so weird. At least, they are no weirder than the rest of us.

In the subsequent chapters of this book, I want to introduce you to what I consider to be the essential pieces for mystical reflection. In chapter 2, I will define mystical experience as a continuum or spectrum which includes many experiences that are easy to overlook. Once we are on the same page on what a mystical experience is, then we can move in chapter 3 to consider the established mystical practices of centering prayer and *lectio Divina*. These are the methods that I blend in a small group setting to create the method of mystical reflection. Pay particular attention to *lectio Divina* here because this practice is used more implicitly and abstractly in mystical reflection than the practice of centering prayer. Chapter 4 contains the method of reflection itself that we used in the pilot mystical reflection groups. I believe that definitions (chapter 2) and method contexts (chapter 3) are vitally important to understand this new method, but if you want to get right down to the heart of the matter, then you can skip ahead to chapter 4 and see the broad brushstrokes of mystical reflection. Chapter 5 consists of my notes and observations on employing the method of mystical reflection in the pilot groups. Also, this chapter has in-depth narratives of meetings and best practices for facilitators. While chapter 4 has the method itself, chapter 5 gives a more richly textured picture of what it is like to have a group mystical reflection session. Proceeding from the picture of an individual session, chapter 6 contains many accounts of mystical experiences from other sources. One of my favorite pieces of the method of mystical reflection is that a group can come together and reflect even if no one in the group has had a new experience. It's just as easy to use an account of a historical mystical experience or one of the many mystical experiences in the Bible. As a result, feel free to use this chapter as a reference tool for both personal and group reflection whenever you like. I've also included quotes and vignettes from the pilot groups themselves in chapter 6; these are real people of today just like you and me, not mystics or saints of bygone eras.

My hope is that we can all see ourselves through each other's eyes and gain the courage to explore in groups together how mystical experiences can deepen and realize our own spiritualities—whether a particular experience happened to each of us or not. In this book, I'm concerned with the pragmatic value of mystical experience. By *pragmatic value*, I mean if mystical experiences really are the touch of the Infinite that most religions claim them to be—not to mention that most religions are built upon the mystical experiences of their founders—then there simply must be some way that one person's mystical experience could directly affect the development of another person's spirituality. Well, let me back up to amend that statement. I'm not saying that there *must* be a way as much as I firmly believe that there *should* be a way. Perhaps, it could look a little bit like this . . .

Chapter 2

What Is a Mystical Experience?

One of the great difficulties of mystical reflection has practically nothing to do with the method of reflection, for defining *mystical experience* brings with it particular challenges. As a result, before we can move to an articulation of the method and its pieces, we're going to have to talk about what mystical experience actually *is*. To do so, let's start with the truly first modern scientific attempt by William James to define mystical experience as a category of experience apart from a specific religious context. Arguably, there are other places where we could start, but I'd like to start here because I feel that it gives us some neutral ground on which to build a foundation. From that point of definition, the rest of this chapter will proceed to reframe the initial criteria of mystical experience into more contemporary terms and introduce my understanding of the mystical experience spectrum.

Williams James and the Four Criteria of Mystical Experience

The first person to articulate a general definition of mystical experience from a scientific, that is social scientific, angle was the great psychologist and philosopher of religion William James. He investigated many aspects of religion in his illustrious career, but

What Is a Mystical Experience?

his masterwork that bears most on our topic here is his chapter on mysticism in *Varieties of Religious Experience* (1902). Up until that time, mystical experience as a *positive* experience was only investigated intrareligiously, i.e., from within a religion. From a scientific perspective, mystical experience was studied chiefly in terms of pathology. James began the conceptual move away from pathologizing mystical experience by focusing on the experience itself as foundational—not doctrine, not religion—simply the experience.

James felt that this approach was the most honest since he did not consider himself a mystic: "Whether my treatment of mystical states will shed more light or darkness, I do not know, for my own constitution shuts me out from their enjoyment almost entirely, and I can speak of them only at second hand."[1] When I first happened upon James's self-reflexive comment, I breathed a sigh of relief. Honestly, I also felt like I had not been privileged with very frequent or obvious mystical experiences. While I have come to define mystical experience more widely, an aspect which I will consider at the end of this chapter, I commiserate with him in the perspective of being on the outside looking in for the vast majority of mystical and religious experiences. While I may now disagree a bit with James concerning the wideness of mystical experience, his self-conscious outsider status helped to set me at ease. My hope is that if you also feel like *mystic* is not a term that describes you, then you will find an inviting space here with William James and me. James's outsider status helps to emphasize the difficulties in defining mystical experience.

James recognized the great difficulty in coming up with one definition that was sufficient to encompass the scope of mystical experience. Consequently, James did not come up with a single definition of mystical experience; instead, he offered a cluster definition in which he denoted four different characteristics of mystical experience which may be present to a lesser or greater degree depending on the individual mystic and situation. Let's dig into those big four as a way to get at what we mean by the term *mystical experience*.

1. James, *Varieties of Religious Experience*, 370.

Briefly stated, James argued for four criteria that define mystical experience: (1) ineffability—the experience resists description, (2) noetic quality—some type of knowledge is imparted through the experience, (3) transiency—the experience itself is fleeting, and (4) passivity—the experience is something that *happens to* a person.[2] Are these characteristics absolutely required in order to label an experience *mystical*? Not exactly. Mystical experiences are as unique and individual as snowflakes; often each one is a universe all to itself. However, since James was trying to lay a foundation for a *scientific* investigation of mystical experiences, one simply has to start somewhere, and he sifted through narratives of mystical experiences to find common points of similarity as a basis for comparison across an ocean of individuality. These four criteria are generally observable when one listens to a great many reports from people who have had a mystical experience, so there is a logic[3] for them to be the baseline for defining what constitutes a mystical experience, as long as that logic is accompanied by the disclaimer that a genuine mystical experience could occur in which not all four criteria are present. Now, with that disclaimer, let's unpack each of those characteristics a bit more and reframe them into contemporary and practical terms in order to wrap our heads around this trait-based definition of mystical experience.

Reframing the Four Criteria for Reflection

(1) Analogy (Replaces Ineffability)

First, ineffability—how on earth do you talk about something that is, by definition, next to impossible to talk about?! Well, like James, we can first admit that mystical experience is exceedingly difficult

---

2. The active part of mysticism is typically known as mystical *practices*, which I briefly defined and disambiguated from mystical *experiences* in the introduction. For more on mystical practices, see Wigner, *Just Begin*, ix–xi, 49–50.

3. This logic is particularly feasible if one is employing a grounded theory approach to the scientific study of mystical experience. See Corbin and Strauss, *Basics of Qualitative Research*, 54–56.

What Is a Mystical Experience?

to describe. Mystical experience is not usually recognized to be a universal type of experience, although it is much more common than generally thought. As pointed out in the Introduction, it is tempting to just say "Well, you have to experience it for yourself," which amounts to saying "You had to be there" when a funny story that you are telling to someone else seemingly falls flat. Is that what we are left with here? I don't think that's the end of the story; rather, I think we can work with this difficulty if we liken it to the development of episodic memory in infants—a process which we *all* definitely go through.

Episodic memory is the subsection of our memories that is concerned with stringing together various events in our lives into coherent strains, or *episodes*, with causes and effects, and it is a type of memory which actually develops over time. Unlike various other types of memory, such as working memory or sense memory, episodic memory is dependent on language acquisition, at least to some extent.[4] So what? What does that interesting factoid have to do with mystical experience? The fact that episodic memory depends on language acquisition explains in large part why most people do not have any memories prior to the age of two, although the actual age after that point varies greatly due to other circumstances as well. To state the matter plainly, we depend on language in order to describe *to ourselves* and others any particular string of events from our past. Before we have enough language facility in order to name/recognize the majority of the objects, persons, and actions in a particular memory, we cannot add those events to our episodic memory in any accessible way to our powers of recall.[5] In other words, we need to be able to describe an experience in order to remember it and communicate it. How does that relate to mystical experience?

---

4. Uehara, "Developmental Changes," 1–2. See also Kamdar, "Infantile Amnesia," 28–30.

5. This process may be unclear to a certain extent due to the common circumstance that earliest memories are often conflated with memories of an older sibling, parent, or family friend retelling the episode.

11

Mystical experience is a unique category of experience, and that uniqueness presents a problem for linguistic description. We do not have a ready store of other experiences to which we can compare it easily. We do not have language skills that directly map to that category of experience, so we run up against the same problem in description of mystical experience that all of us had with all types of experiences in our earliest childhood. Still, we are not children barely learning language at this point, so what can we do? We can speak about an indescribable experience through the linguistic device that we have learned to use for other unique experiences: *analogy*. While ineffability is more accurately descriptive as a characteristic, the term *analogy* is far more useful to remind each of us of how we *can* talk about this category of experience, not of how we *cannot* talk about it.

Why is the presence of analogy important for either describing your own mystical experiences or fruitfully listening to others describe their experiences? Analogy is important here for two vital reasons. First, we can look for the use of analogies when someone is describing a mystical experience and use analogies ourselves when searching to describe our own mystical experiences. If we see analogy as a go-to method to talk about mystical experiences, then the indescribable is made the tiniest bit more describable. Second, recognition of the strident presence of analogy in historical descriptions of mystical experiences helps to explain why mystical experiences seem to appear in so much variety from person to person and religion to religion. In the same way, whenever we analogize an indescribable experience with other more common experiences in our lives, we will always run the risk of using an experience or image that another person does not share or cannot easily relate to.

If we forget to look at descriptions of mystical experiences in terms of analogy, then we can miss entirely that a certain experience of ours may indeed be mystical because it simply doesn't sound as fantastic as the descriptions recounted by various other mystics throughout the ages. Realizing that these descriptions are actually analogies for the most part may clarify matters significantly. For

What Is a Mystical Experience?

instance, I have never watched a bush burn, so if a mystic were to offer an analogy to me that his experience was a bush burning that was never fully burned up,[6] then I might get lost in the analogy. Possibly, I might even think that I have never had a mystical experience since my personal experiences don't add up to the intensity of his description. While we cannot look for ineffability, we can be on the lookout for analogy, and that gives us something we can latch onto. Additionally, analogy gives us a tool to assist us with the always imprecise task of trying to describe the ineffable.

(2) Perspective (Replaces Noetic Quality)

Second, noetic quality, William James's term, means that mystical experience imparts knowledge. Let's start with the term itself here. Why call this criterion *noetic quality* instead of the far more relatable term *knowledge*? That semantic anomaly gives us a clue to the difficulty in this trait. Account after account of mystical experience shares that some type of knowledge was communicated in the encounter: an experiential knowledge, a knowledge *beyond* words, and, often, even beyond concepts. In the Christian tradition, this knowledge imparted purely through mystical experience and reflection on that experience goes by the descriptive metaphor of "the cloud of unknowing."[7] Without any suitable words to section off this category of knowledge from *all* other types, those ancient mystics felt that the only appropriate term was *un*-knowing.

James's noetic quality tries to capture the heart of this difficulty while still labeling a category for study. Often, as you'll likely see in your mystical reflection groups, the very fact that an experience is mystical brings up this criterion. It is something "you

6. Exod 3:1–3.

7. *Cloud of Unknowing*, 256: "For no matter how much spiritual understanding a man may have in the knowledge of all created spiritual things, he can never, by the work of his understanding, arrive at the knowledge of an uncreated spiritual thing, which is nothing except God. But by the failing of it, he can. For where his understanding fails is in nothing except God alone; and it was for this reason that Saint Denis [Pseudo-Dionysius] said, 'The truly divine knowledge of God is that which is known by unknowing.'"

just *know*" or that "you had to be there" to understand. We have already considered this problem with respect to ineffability/analogy, but this criterion approaches the difficulty from a more internal angle. If possible, I think noetic quality might be even harder to grasp as a concept than ineffability.

In view of this difficulty, I want to offer a term and action that is even more utilitarian to replace James's original. Think of noetic quality not as some mysterious, elusive knowledge or even unknowing; instead, think of it as *perspective*. By perspective, I mean that a mystical experience commonly doesn't impart new facts of one type or another; rather, mystical experience serves to set the whole of the person's life in a new framework—to see life with a new or additionally faceted viewpoint—a *perspective* shift. When you are talking about mystical experiences in your groups or reading accounts of mystical experiences, don't listen for clouds of unknowing, noetic qualities, or the secrets of the universe. Listen for a change in perspective.

(3) Fleeting (Replaces Transiency)

Next, transiency is the third criterion of mystical experience according to James. Honestly, this is probably the easiest one to observe and explain. Succinctly stated, mystical experiences do not last very long; they are *fleeting*. Many experiences happen in seconds—or the ticks between seconds—and few mystical experiences last longer than an hour. While accounts certainly exist about mystical experiences that are lengthier, they are far more rare. In fact, one of the most basic ways that one may tell that a mystical experience has occurred is the short space of feeling different in a day full of regular happenings. As a result, I don't have much to say here by way of reframing other than renaming *transiency* as the more contemporary adjective *fleeting*.

While the adjective *fleeting* is understandable, it applies in two distinct ways to mystical experience: to the experience itself and to the feelings which may accompany the experience. Literally speaking, it is quite common that one's perception of time

What Is a Mystical Experience?

shifts during the experience. A few minutes may be experienced as feeling like several hours. Conversely, one's perception of time may speed up to display the appearance of having lost time. Differing perceptions of time proliferate when you bring in the consideration of dreams as mystical experiences as well. No matter how you slice it, changes in the perception of time are common and obvious features of many mystical experiences. However, the second way in which *fleeting* applies to mystical experiences is a less obvious connection which, rather paradoxically, is far more important to expect.

I feel that the adjective *fleeting* should also be applied to the feelings that immediately follow a mystical experience. While it is not universal, many people who have had mystical experiences report a lingering feeling of difference after the experience, such as: a sense of the presence of God, a connection to other living beings, or awareness of the significance of actions and relationships. These feelings are wonderful. If they accompany a mystical experience for you, then embrace them, enjoy them, celebrate them; but do not expect them to last forever. These feelings are fleeting, although they often last much longer than the experience itself. I want to emphasize this last point because one shouldn't feel like a failure when these feelings fade. It is the nature of these types of experiences. Mystical experiences stand out as singular in our lives, but the sheer bulk of ordinary experience can crowd out the poignancy of those brief moments. Perspective, as mentioned above, may remain shifted, but feelings associated with mystical experiences are squarely placed under the adjective *fleeting*. The feelings of a moment are no less beautiful if they are brief; it could be argued that they are even more beautiful because they are fleeting. So, mystical experiences often—though not always—share the characteristic criteria of transiency (fleeting), a noetic quality (perspective), and ineffability (analogy). Along with these characteristics, mystical experiences typically share the trait of passivity on the part of the person in the mystical moment.

(4) Unpredictability (Replaces Passivity)

James's final criterion of mystical experience is *passivity*, a term which may be easily misunderstood today. Perhaps, a better term for this characteristic is *unpredictability*. In other words, mystical experiences happen to people. No one does or makes a mystical experience. It is unpredictable. In fact, in a number of religious traditions the very act of trying to have a mystical experience will preclude the possibility of an authentic encounter with the divine. Of all the criteria described by James, this final one requires the least reframing. Still, I would like to emphasize two points concerning the unpredictable nature of mystical experience which James points out in his original discussion.

First, unpredictability refers to a mystical experience as an *event*, but that criterion also calls attention to the role of mystical practices in relation to mystical experience. A mystical experience happens to someone, but that does not mean that one has to sit passively waiting for the unforeseen mystical moment. The predictable aspect is simply located *before* and *after* the mystical experience. James notes that a mystical experience "may be facilitated by preliminary voluntary operations, as by fixing the attention, or going through certain bodily performances, or in other ways which manuals of mysticism prescribe."[8] In this book, and in my earlier book *Just Begin*, I refer to these preliminaries as mystical or spiritual practices. "Preliminaries" is a poorly descriptive term for mystical practices, since they shape and develop the spiritual life of a person far beyond their connection to a mystical experience. In fact, mystical practices can lead to a richly edifying life even if one *never* has a mystical experience of an obvious sort. These practices help to prepare one to recognize a mystical experience when or if it happens, and typically they provide some context for help in interpreting them. Consequently, if you're looking for something that you can *do* while you're waiting for that unpredictable experience to happen to you, then look no further than mystical practices, but they are more than time-fillers. You can build a rich spiritual

---

8. James, *Varieties of Religious Experience*, 372.

What Is a Mystical Experience?

life through the regular use of mystical practices alone; mystical experience is not intended to be treated similarly. One of the main purposes of this book is to point out that the mystical experience is not the end goal of the spiritual life. It is a step along the way, and it is a step intended to be taken in relation to others. This line of thinking also extends to the place of reflection and interpretation in connection to mystical experiences.

Second, while the mystical experience may indeed be passive and unpredictable, it does not have a passive effect on one's life; rather, it creates an interruption which must be addressed.

James touches on this point when he mentions, "Mystical states, strictly so-called, are never merely interruptive. Some memory of their content always remains, and a profound sense of their importance. They modify the inner life of the subject between the times of their recurrence."[9] This statement sounds quite a bit like the noetic quality of James's second criterion, but he is not pointing out here that the mystical experience changes one's perspective. Instead, he is emphasizing the interruptive aspect of such a unique, unpredictable experience. It creates a break in one's life that must be addressed, must be explored. This interruptive quality makes interpretation essential, which is why I think that mystical reflection in small groups is especially necessary. Perhaps the experiencer has the resource of one-on-one spiritual direction, but, if not, my method is an alternative, and it is an alternative that is meant to affect directly those beyond the experiencer him- or herself.

To reiterate before moving on to a final essential aspect in defining mystical experience, William James has designated four primary criteria of mystical experience: ineffability, noetic quality, transiency, and passivity. While these terms are academically instructive, they are not as easy to understand as they once were. As a result, reframing them is necessary for relevancy through the concepts of analogy, perspective, fleeting, and unpredictability. From this discussion of descriptive characteristics, let's now transition to consider mystical experience in a way which James

9. James, *Varieties of Religious Experience*, 372.

intimates but never labels specifically. To complete the definition fully, let's proceed to consider mystical experiences along a *continuum* or *spectrum* of experience rather than as discrete events with these four recognizable, recurring features.

Mystical Spectrum

We hear a lot about spectrums, or spectra, these days. There is the gender spectrum, the sexuality spectrum, the autism spectrum, and, of course, the color spectrum. It seems that there is a spectrum for almost everything, and I sincerely believe that is a wonderful circumstance. We spend too much time in this world trying to shoehorn objects, tasks, ideas, and people into black-and-white extremes. Why? There is so much middle ground to go around. Among all of these spectrums, I want to delineate another one: *the mystical experience spectrum*. As we have been following William James in this chapter, I want to point out that James did not designate a spectrum for mystical experience. He saw mystical experiences lying along a *continuum*, although he did not use that term specifically. While I do prefer the term *spectrum*, and I will explain exactly why I prefer that term subsequently, James's descriptions of the variety of mystical experiences can help us as a place to begin to widen out the range of this type of experience.

William James proposes six stages along the mystical experience spectrum.[10] First, he initiates the spectrum with the moment of sudden insight—the epiphany moment—when the proverbial light bulb turns on over our heads. If you have ever had a moment where the solution to a problem or a new idea suddenly appeared to you, then—congratulations—you're on the spectrum. Second, have you ever been moved by a speech, work of literature, poetry, or music (and I would add movies too)? If so, then—congratulations—you're on the spectrum. Third, have you ever had a sense of *déjà vu*?[11] If so, then—congratulations—you're on the spectrum.

---

10. James, *Varieties of Religious Experience*, 373–76.
11. Have you ever had a sense of *déjà vu*?

What Is a Mystical Experience?

Fourth, have you ever had a fleeting moment of connection to all things? Perhaps, you had such a moment during quiet contemplation or thrilling exhilaration?[12] If so, then—congratulations—you're on the spectrum. Fifth, have you ever had a profound sense of wonder, awe, or dread that you just couldn't explain? If so, then—congratulations—you're on the spectrum. Sixth, and finally for James, have you ever had an extreme state of mystical consciousness? Here is where we locate "traditional" mystical experiences of dreams, visions, prophecies, enlightenments, and burning bushes. If so, then—congrat . . . well, you probably already knew you were on the spectrum with that one. Honestly, I think we can expand this list out even further to many moments of connection and community *in relationships*; James opts for mostly individual examples in his book. The point of James, and the important takeaway for us, is that mystical experience is not just about the fantastic and unknown. It's about seeing the mysterious in the ordinary just as much, if not more, than waiting for the extraordinary.

Now, in light of these stages, let's turn to a distinction between James's stages as part of a continuum and the idea of spectrum as we will view it here. While this issue may seem to be semantics for some, I do think a vital point rests here. In delineating mystical experiences along a continuum of six stages, if we go exactly with James, then we may be biased to see mystical experience as a *linear* progression. In other words, we might implicitly and unconsciously expect mystical experiences in our lives to look like this:

START	GETTING BETTER	!! WINNER !!
Insight → Moved by a poem → *Deja vu* → Sense of connection → Wonder → Visions!		

Mystical experiences do not operate according to nice and neat linear rules. Some people will have many of these types of mystical experience in this order. For others, they will be in another order, or stages will be missing. For still others, all of this may start at visions and dreams and backtrack from there. James's stages are

---

12. At this point, many religions and faith traditions view sexual experience as such a connection, i.e., "two become one" (Gen 2:24).

19

intended to offer a range of experience, not a pattern to follow. Consequently, I think that the concept of a spectrum, and the metaphor of the color spectrum, is much closer to how mystical experiences actually appear:

Much like the mnemonic device for the rainbow, *Roy G. Biv* (red, orange, yellow, green, blue, indigo, and violet), no one stage of mystical experience, as outlined by James, is better than another one. It would be like arguing that red is a better color than yellow or green. In other words, all the colors and shades of mystical experience are legitimate, valuable, and worthy of reflection.

Before moving on to a discussion of the background mystical practices that form the structure of group mystical reflection, let's revisit for clarity's sake the different pieces of a working definition of mystical experience. We have walked along in this chapter with William James to describe a mystical experience through the traits of ineffability, noetic quality, transiency, and passivity. Since these terms have become somewhat archaic, we have reframed these traits through analogy, perspective, fleeting, and unpredictability. Mystical experiences can be described only by analogy, often lead to a new perspective, are fleeting in length of time, and happen to a person unpredictably. Along with these foundational characteristics, we then proceeded to journey with and beyond James to open up mystical experiences to a much wider spectrum of life than burning bushes and bodhi trees. If you would like more specific examples of mystical experiences of fantastic and ordinary

What Is a Mystical Experience?

varieties, we will turn to historical accounts of mystical experiences in chapter 6. For now, let's proceed to discuss the mystical practices of centering prayer and *lectio Divina*, for they are the basis on which I have constructed the method of mystical reflection for groups and individuals.

CHAPTER 3

Lectio Divina and Centering Prayer

By now, hopefully, we are on the same page concerning the need for mystical reflection (chapter 1) and concerning exactly what the term *mystical experience* means (chapter 2). If so, then why not jump right into the method of mystical reflection? Feel free to skip ahead to the next chapter, if you like, but this chapter on the mystical practices of *lectio Divina* and centering prayer is not functionless window dressing. These practices are spiritually enriching in their own right without any connection to mystical experience, and I recommend experimenting with and exploring them on your own, regardless of how you connect them to mystical experiences and mystical reflection. Additionally, I have found *lectio* and centering to be ideal mystical practices to use fruitfully in a group context. They are easy to learn and start using, and they have many variations which offer great potential for spiritual growth in almost endless permutations. However, more directly to the point here, these established spiritual practices show the *practical* foundations of the method of mystical reflection, even as previous chapters dealt with theoretical foundations. Mystical reflection is not a spiritual practice conjured out of thin air; rather, it is historically rooted in two of the most productive and meaningful Christian spiritual practices: *lectio Divina* and centering prayer.

While we'll move to a brief introduction and step-by-step application of each practice in the next sections, I want to emphasize some benefits from grounding mystical reflection on these two bases. First, if you have previous experience with either *lectio* or centering, then those skills are transferrable to mystical reflection. Now, if you have not practiced, or even heard of, these mystical practices before, fear not because I will give you all the background context you need in order to move on to mystical reflection. However, whether experienced in *lectio* and centering or not, you can partake of the next advantage. Specifically, as a second benefit, there are many manuals, textbooks, and how-to instructions for both *lectio* and centering. Please refer to the end of this chapter for a list of recommended sources for going further with these practices. *Lectio* and centering have been used in multiple contexts, both individual and communal, so you have, through these practices, access to more informational material than just what is set before you in this book. There is always more to learn. Now, without further ado, let's dig into the methods of *lectio Divina* and centering prayer.

Lectio Divina

Lectio Divina, or sacred/divine reading, can be defined most simply as a mystical practice about how one reads sacred texts, principally the Bible. In this practice, a participant selects a portion of a reading and then reads through it multiple times. Each reading has a specific purpose beyond comprehending the historical meaning of the text. The practice helps one to meditate, or concentrate, on Scripture in order for one to gain insight and/or meet God. It is a simple practice to begin step-by-step, but there are many, many variations built on this basic framework.

Thinking Spiritually in Small Groups

How to Practice

1. The first stage of the practice is *lectio* (lit. "reading"). In this stage, choose a Scripture passage, or some other spiritually meaningful reading, and *read* it slowly and repetitively. You may choose a different reading for each session.
2. The second stage is *oratio* (lit. "speaking"). In this stage, read the passage *aloud*. Focus on what God is saying to you. Look for a specific word, phrase, analogy, or image that stands out or "shimmers" to you.[1] It does not have to be one of the main content pieces of the passage. It can be any part of the passage.
3. The third stage is *meditatio* (lit. "thinking" or "concentrating"). In this stage, *concentrate* on the word, phrase, analogy, or image that stood out to you when you were reading. Focus on how God could be speaking to you today through this word, phrase, analogy, or image. You then end your prayer time with the Lord's Prayer, or another personally meaningful prayer, and keep concentrating on what stood out to you from your reading throughout the day.
4. The final stage is *contemplatio* (lit. "contemplation").[2] This stage is something you cannot control. This is where God *meets* you, and it can happen any time or anywhere. The process of *lectio* helps one to be attentive to those rather subtle "Eureka!" moments when an insight strikes you suddenly, because God is not limited to showing up in only obvious and fantastic ways.

   1. While I am using the word *shimmer* in a primarily analogical way here, I have often had people relate to me this specific effect in a literal sense too. Another common visual phenomenon is for the word or phrase to seem brighter while the surrounding text seems dim or fuzzy. Of course, you do not have to have this experience in order to select a word or have a meaningful *lectio Divina* session.
   2. There is a long history for the word *contemplation* in Christian spirituality. Suffice it to say, in contemporary terms, the words *illumination* or *enlightenment* would be much closer to what is meant here than how the word *contemplation* is generally used today.

That's it. Those are the four basic stages of *lectio Divina*. As I mentioned previously, they are the basis for almost endless variation. To investigate some of those endless variations along with common questions and answers that crop up when first exploring this practice, you may want to take a look at where I have treated *lectio* in my previous book on mystical practices.[3] *Lectio* forms one practical starting point for the foundation for mystical reflection; centering prayer serves as the other part of that origin.

Centering Prayer

As centering prayer is much newer then *lectio Divina*, at least as a discrete practice, let's begin with a little bit of historical background. Thomas Keating and M. Basil Pennington were the first to define centering prayer; however, they noted points of contact between this prayer method, Thomas Merton, and the historic practice of contemplative prayer.[4] Centering prayer was offered by Keating[5] and Pennington in the 1970s and 1980s as both a gateway toward contemplative prayer and as an alternative to the then-popular practice of transcendental meditation.[6] While contemplative prayer has been practiced for millennia in Christian monasteries and convents, it was typically taught only as a total lifestyle commitment. Centering prayer offers a simple step-by-step method to enter into the contemplative silences that are at the heart of Christian monasticism.

---

3. Wigner, *Just Begin*, 13–20, 204–7.

4. In Christian history, the term *contemplative prayer* was often used as a catch-all term for many aspects of the spiritual life or way of contemplation. Particularly, *contemplative prayer* was used in a manner which would make it synonymous with the term *mystical experience* as presented in this book.

5. Keating, *Open Mind, Open Heart*, 139–41.

6. See Forem, *Transcendental Meditation*.

How to Practice

1. In the practice of centering prayer, you ideally section off two twenty-minute periods of time a day to pray. In that time, you sit quietly, not attempting to speak or ask God anything; rather, your intention is simply to remain present before God.
2. Choose a word that is personally meaningful to you as a reminder to seek God within. In other words, choose a single word or short phrase to remind yourself of God whenever you realize that your mind has wandered off during prayer. Try not to change the word too often, especially during the prayer time. You can use practically any word, including *God, love, hope, mercy,* or *mystery*.
3. Next, sit comfortably with your eyes closed, and breathe slowly in and out of your nose for a minute or two to settle yourself down. You could also pray a short introductory prayer, such as "For God alone, my soul in silence waits. Truly, my hope is in him" (Ps 62:6). Then, quietly introduce the word you have chosen to remind you of God.
4. Continue sitting silently for twenty minutes, listening to the silence. When thoughts begin to arise, just repeat your word aloud or think it silently.
5. At the end of the prayer period, remain in silence with eyes closed for a few moments. Reciting the Lord's Prayer slowly is a good way to return your thoughts to the world around you. You might also want to get up and walk around for a few moments rather than immediately beginning a new task in order to reorient yourself.

As you are practicing this prayer, keep these practical points in mind:

1. The recommended time for this prayer is twenty minutes. Keating and Pennington suggest two periods each day: one first thing in the morning and the other in the afternoon or

Lectio Divina and Centering Prayer

early evening. However, don't let time be what stops you. If you can do only five minutes, then do five minutes. On the other hand, you might find the practice so valuable, or your thoughts so hard to tame, that you want to spend longer.

2. Your prayer word is not a mantra. You are not trying to repeat it as often as possible or to drive out all conscious thought through its repetition. It is a reminder to you whenever you have noticed that your mind has drifted. The word is not your focus. It is an aid to help your mind stay in one place for the prayer period.

3. The end of the prayer period can be signaled by an alarm. A relatively quiet alarm is helpful not to jar you out of the prayer time.

4. Unlike many forms of meditation, the goal of centering prayer is not particularly about being as still as possible. If you need to shift your position or scratch an itch, do so. Just try not to make a habit of fidgeting. Also, as you pray, you might become more aware of your body sensations. While that awareness can be interesting, it is not the goal of the practice. Simply note your observation and then proceed back to your word.

The effects of centering prayer occur most noticeably outside of the prayer time, but they are subtle results—increasing calmness, patience, an inner stillness. Don't try to make your prayer time perfect. Just try to be consistent. God sees your effort and loves you for it.

That's the method of centering prayer. You may notice that it is a little more specific than *lectio*. This aspect is due in part to its relatively recent distillation as a discrete mystical practice, and, as you may surmise, this characteristic also figures into how we will be using centering prayer within the larger method of mystical reflection. However, just like with *lectio Divina* above, if you would like to dig further into centering prayer, then you can find variations of the practice along with frequently asked questions and answers to those questions in my previous book *Just Begin*.[7] After one final comment on how *lectio* and centering interact in the formation of mystical reflection, we can proceed to a discussion of the new method itself.

Macro and Micro Levels

Before moving on, I want to draw attention to the relative utilization of *lectio* and centering individually within mystical reflection. It is not an even 50/50 split. They serve different purposes in my new method. Think of it like this: one is structural in an overarching way, and the other is structural in a narrowed, focused way. *Lectio Divina* as a method is the basic framework for the whole method of mystical reflection. While it might be a little simplistic, one could say that mystical reflection is *lectio Divina* in a group where the "text" for reflection is an individual's mystical experience. So, if you are already practiced in using *lectio*, then the overall structure of mystical reflection will feel very familiar. Conversely, I employ centering prayer in a more laser-like manner because, during two of the steps of the method of mystical reflection, group participants actually engage in short centering prayer sessions. As we move to the full delineation of mystical reflection in the next chapter, try to keep that procedural split in mind: *lectio* on the macro level and centering on the micro level. While they have different functions, centering prayer and *lectio Divina* share space as the collective taproot for the new method of mystical reflection, planting it in the fertile ground of historic Christian spirituality.

Resources for Further Study on *Lectio Divina* and Centering Prayer

Lectio Divina

Benner, David G. *Opening to God:* Lectio Divina *and Life as Prayer*. Downers Grove, IL: InterVarsity, 2010.

---

7. Wigner, *Just Begin*, 52–56, 213–15.

Lectio Divina and Centering Prayer

Bianchi, Enzo. *Lectio Divina: From God's Word to Our Lives.* Brewster, MA: Paraclete, 2015.
Casey, Michael. *Sacred Reading: The Ancient Art of Lectio Divina.* Ligouri, MO: Ligouri, 1995.
Earle, Mary C. *Broken Body, Healing Spirit: Lectio Divina and Living with Illness.* Harrisburg, PA: Morehouse, 2003.
Hall, Thelma. *Too Deep for Words: Rediscovering Lectio Divina.* New York: Paulist, 1998.
Johnson, Jan. *Meeting God in Scripture: A Hands-On Guide to Lectio Divina.* Oxford, UK: Monarch, 2016.
Paintner, Christine Valters. *Lectio Divina—The Sacred Art: Transforming Words and Images into Heart-Centered Prayer.* Woodstock, VT: SkyLight, 2011.
Paintner, Christine Valters, and Lucy Wynkoop. *Lectio Divina: Contemplative Awakening and Awareness.* New York: Paulist, 2008.
Pennington, M. Basil. *Lectio Divina: Renewing the Ancient Practice of Praying the Scriptures.* New York: Crossroad, 1998.
———. *Living in the Question: Meditations in the Style of Lectio Divina.* New York: Continuum, 1999.
Studzinski, Raymond. *Reading to Live: The Evolving Practice of Lectio Divina.* Trappist, KY: Liturgical, 2009.

Centering Prayer

Bourgeault, Cynthia. *Centering Prayer and Inner Awakening.* Cambridge, MA: Cowley, 2004.
———. *The Heart of Centering Prayer: Nondual Christianity in Theory and Practice.* Boulder, CO: Shambhala, 2016.
Frenette, David. *The Path of Centering Prayer: Deepening Your Experience of God.* Boulder, CO: Sounds True, 2012.
Keating, Thomas. *Divine Therapy and Addiction: Centering Prayer and the Twelve Steps.* New York: Lantern, 2011.
———. *Open Mind, Open Heart: The Contemplative Dimension of the Gospel.* 1986. Reprint. New York: Continuum, 2002.
Lawson, Paul David. *Old Wine in New Skins: Centering Prayer and Systems Theory.* New York: Lantern, 2001.
Muyskens, J. David. *Sacred Breath: Forty Days of Centering Prayer.* Nashville: Upper Room, 2010.
O'Madagain, Murchadh. *Centering Prayer and the Healing of the Unconscious.* New York: Lantern, 2007.
Pennington, M. Basil. *Call to the Center: The Gospel's Invitation to Deeper Prayer.* Hyde Park, NY: New City, 1995.
———. *Centering Prayer: Renewing an Ancient Christian Prayer Form.* Garden City, NY: Doubleday, 1980.

Reininger, Gustave, ed. *Centering Prayer in Daily Life and Ministry*. New York: Continuum, 1998.
———. *The Diversity of Centering Prayer*. New York: Continuum, 1999.
Smith, Elizabeth, and Joseph Chalmers. *A Deeper Love: An Introduction to Centering Prayer*. New York: Continuum, 1999.
Ward, Thomas R. *Centering Prayer*. Cincinnati: Forward Movement, 1997.

CHAPTER 4

The Method of Mystical Reflection

Now that the necessary scaffolding of the previous chapters is in place—the rationale for why mystical reflection is necessary (chapter 1), an explanation of the full spectrum of mystical experiences (chapter 2), and the bare bones of centering prayer and *lectio Divina* (chapter 3)—we can proceed here to mark out the exact structure of the method of mystical reflection. Incidentally, if you were pressed for time and skipped to this point, then you can start using the method in your group, and you can backtrack to read about the underlying context of mystical reflection later. Let's first see the steps themselves as outline points, and I'll then go into greater explanatory depths of each piece:

1. Settling into the Space
2. Prayer for Guidance
3. First Telling/Reading of a Mystical Experience (ME)
4. First Centering Prayer Period
5. Second Telling/Reading of a Mystical Experience (ME)
6. Second Centering Prayer Period
7. Sharing Time
8. Ending Prayer for Guidance and Parting

As noted in the previous chapter, you may glimpse in these numbered steps that the method of mystical reflection mimics the rhythms of *lectio Divina*—reading, breathing, sitting silently, reading again, and so forth. Centering prayer is more directly utilized in mystical reflection, but the structure of *lectio Divina* undergirds the whole. With this rhythmic structure in mind, let's take a deeper look at each individual step in the method.

Step 1: Settling into the Space

On the surface, settling can take the form of five to ten minutes of chitchat, but there is some deep structure to this stage beyond the simple surface that is essential foundation for the method to be successful. First, settling into the space can happen only if setting up the space is a concern from the outset. Consider having the group meet in the home of one or more of the group members, perhaps on a rotating basis, in order to avoid an imposition on a single person or family. Please feel free to experiment and customize mystical reflection to whatever your particular group's composition finds helpful, but I have found, in all types of small group work, that meeting in homes is invaluable in creating a relaxed sense of community. To meet in homes will likely require some extra work in aligning schedules, considering the possibility of childcare,[1] etc., but it is time well spent. A comfortable space is an essential ingredient in creating a safe space, and a safe space is essential when you will be broaching something as personal and sensitive as a mystical experience.

Second, I recommend sharing a meal together whenever possible. Don't underestimate the value of eating together. It seems like a small thing, but it has often been the "make or break" point in

---

1. If your group includes parents with small children, I urge you to find some possibility for childcare. While children can deeply enrich the gathering and meal times of a meeting, I have found it next to impossible to make sure that young kids are quiet enough for the group to enter the times of silence necessitated by this method. Honestly, I don't think it's fair to lay such a burden of silence on children below a certain age (e.g., ten or twelve).

The Method of Mystical Reflection

small groups which I have facilitated. Also, it helps when members all bring something to contribute to the meal, or there is a rotating responsibility for "home cooking." This aspect may not work with every group, but the authenticity of the meal often sets the stage for a relaxed and intimate gathering of friends—not just participants. Eating together in homes is a sure way to work toward the safe space where persons can open up to others concerning the intimacy of an ME with a realization that mystical reflection is also an intimate task first and foremost, not an analytical one.

You may notice at this point that a lot of time and effort may go into setting up the space before we can even think about implementing the actual method. Settling into the space through conversation and eating together also takes up the bulk of the time for each meeting. Typically, I have allowed a two-hour window for the practice of mystical reflection, but the method itself seldom lasts longer than thirty minutes. That is an intentional choice. Experiment with what works for you, but I advise you not to run past these recommendations too quickly. They are simple things, but they are investments with a great return. Also, you will likely find that it takes time for a group to prepare to go deep in the way mystical reflection requires. A slow buildup to the method creates the right attitude among group members as well as the right atmosphere in the space.

After this long process of settling in, to officially open the method, I have used a couple of different entry transitions. First, if all of you have shared a meal, then it is helpful to physically transition to another space to prepare bodily to shift gears in thinking, conversing, and praying. For instance, you all could move from the kitchen or dining room to the living room or the backyard. Second, it helps to have a mechanism to shift conversation deeper while everyone is affirmed as a worthwhile member of the group. To accomplish this task, I like to employ some version of a check-in. Most basically, the facilitator could simply ask "How has everyone's week been?" and go around the group, allowing for a one- or two-minute response from each person. Time may be adjusted depending on the size of the group, and the possibility not to share needs to be offered to participants as well. Additionally, as your group meets over time, allow for check-in to expand because it may also become a necessary time for group members to share how the last meeting's mystical reflection impacted them since then. In that vein, this process of check-in naturally brings the first step of settling into the space to a close and proceeds toward deeper mystical reflection through the use of some type of prayer of guidance as the next methodological step.

Step 2: Prayer for Guidance

After check-in has allowed everyone to settle down and begin to look introspectively at their own experiences, I like to begin mystical reflection proper with a prayer for guidance. Personally, I prefer a fixed prayer at this stage because I feel that it aids people in getting into the spiritual and emotional groove of what we're about to do. My preferred prayer is Prayer 57, "For Guidance," from the *Book of Common Prayer*:[2]

> Direct us, O Lord, in all our doings with *thy* most gracious favor, and further us with *thy* continual help; that in all our works begun, continued, and ended in *thee*, we may glorify *thy* holy Name, and finally, by *thy* mercy, obtain everlasting life; through Jesus Christ our Lord. Amen.

In your group, you may want to experiment with this prayer, another written prayer, or extemporaneous prayer of some sort. Feel free to customize and make it your own. The point of the mystical reflection method is not to follow the exact mechanics of each step; rather, the point is to facilitate an honest and fruitful sharing of an ME with others—so that it can enrich the spirituality of all who are present. However you get to that point is *the* right way for you, so don't be afraid to make some mistakes on the way to getting there.

---

2. "For Guidance" (Prayer 57), in Howe, *Book of Common Prayer*, 832. I like to update *thy* and *thee* with *your* and *you*.

The Method of Mystical Reflection

One additional note concerning this step is a bit more theological and philosophical in tone. While on a practical level this prayer serves as an opening to mystical reflection and an additional aid to settling the group into a deeper place of reflection, there is a more important spiritual activity going on here. In the first step, through check-in, you are inviting each member of the group into the experience and valuing their individual experiences, mystical or not, that occurred in the course of a given week. In this second step, you are all inviting God into the process as well. Mystical reflection is not just about reflection on a time or event when God *did* speak. It is also about a recognition and belief that God *does* speak and an expectation that God may indeed speak right *now*. A prayer of guidance may seem like such a small thing, and it can be if treated flippantly, but it has the potential to be a deep spiritual practice of its own. When words and intention meet an attitude of expectation, the members of the group are better prepared for whatever may happen in that time of mystical reflection—no matter how mysterious such happenings may be (cf. Isa 55:8–9). Consequently, once *all* human and divine participants have been invited, then it is time to begin telling the story of the ME for the meeting.

Step 3: First Telling/Reading of a Mystical Experience (ME)

Mystical reflection begins in earnest at this step with one person choosing the ME to tell or read to others for the meeting. I find it most helpful to set up an agreed-upon rotation by the first or second meeting of the group and stick to that schedule as much as possible for multiple meetings. In this way, it will give each person plenty of time to prepare to share an ME with others. While a few members may be eager to jump in and share, others will definitely need time to gather their thoughts and grapple with how to put such an indescribable experience into words. I also encourage you to hold this schedule lightly; there is nothing wrong with shifting the schedule to fit the busy lives and individual events of a group.

Thinking Spiritually in Small Groups

While I do urge an exploratory and experimental attitude in mystical reflection to allow for your group to go organically in the direction that works best, there are two actions which I consider indispensable in this step. First, I do find it absolutely essential during the readings/tellings of an ME that there are no comments or cross talk. Except for the sharer, all other participants are just to listen actively. Let the story of the ME wash over you. You're not trying to "get it" or "receive" anything yet. Just listen and be. At this juncture, some may think, "Well, what if I have clarifying questions?" That's fine, but this step is not the time for it. There will be a time for questions of that nature in connection with the second telling/reading. However, just listening the first time should be treated by the group as sacrosanct. Second, I recommend having only one ME related for each meeting. Reflecting deeply on an ME will take a lot more energy than most suppose. Give each experience its full moment in sharp focus. It also is helpful to concentrate, at least in the beginning, on MEs that are discrete events rather than, say, a mystical mood that suffused someone's life for a longer span of time. These pieces are really the only ones which I consider to be essential and nonnegotiable for the method, but there are several other areas in this step that allow for experimentation and customization either within the group as a whole or on an individual basis.[3]

It often comes as a surprise to others that I do not require each ME for reflection to be the actual experience of the person sharing for the meeting. While personal MEs will likely predominate your group meetings, there is nothing wrong with a person selecting a historical ME from a recognized mystic or even relating a tale concerning an ME that happened to one's friends or family. You can find a variety of MEs that I've gathered together in the sixth chapter of this book for that specific purpose. Especially if

---

3. Of course, by "nonnegotiable," I mean that I find them almost deceptively important and vital to the success of the method. However, try to remain always open to the needs of the group. Sharing indescribable experiences about meeting the invisible plane, ultimate reality, or the divine is not an exact science. Allow space for the "art" of the task to grow and emerge on its own. The only real essential is to *keep at it*.

The Method of Mystical Reflection

your group meets often or over a long period of time, you'll have sessions in which no one has experienced a new ME. That's great. This method is specifically designed to help anyone reflect on MEs that are not their own as food for their own spirituality and as a gateway for new experiences with the divine. As a result, any ME should be able to fill the bill for reflection, not just the ones nearest to each of us.

A similar point of customization rests with how the ME itself is communicated: prepared in advance or spontaneous. In the groups that I have facilitated, some persons wrote their experiences down and read them. Others spoke extemporaneously. While I am definitely the type of person that *needs* to have a write-up in front of me, I discovered that, on balance, both ways worked, but each way had advantages and disadvantages. On the plus side for writing, since the method recommends going over the ME twice, due to its similarity to *lectio Divina*, a write-up of an ME helps for standardization. As we'll see in a moment, during the second reading, you'll be paying attention to what words, phrases, or images stand out to you. That process is typically easier if you hear the exact same account twice. Now, on the side of simply telling the story, what may be lost in standardization is typically compensated for with emotional resonance. In other words, when someone spoke their story they engaged the full range of nonverbal communication, particularly in the first telling. Also, I did have more than one participant tell me that they simply couldn't write it down. There was no way to capture the event in written words, and it was difficult enough through spoken words. I recommend offering both options and paying attention to what works best in the group, but I would caution against ever completely requiring either spoken or written format. Such a restriction can be too confining in an activity that needs the maximum amount of room to breathe and be free.

These few paragraphs stress my only general recommendations for what is essential and what is customizable, but feel free to take experimentation further. In the groups which I have facilitated, there was always a component of telling or reading an ME,

37

but not all MEs are sufficiently linear in order to be communicable in this fashion. Be open to the utilization of poetry, visual art, dance, video, metaphor—even as MEs can show up in the most unlooked-for places during the least likely times, communicating them to others may have to take some real outside-the-box thinking. Don't be afraid to try something different.[4] Now, once the sharer has completed the first reading, telling, or some form of communicating the ME, the entire group will move into a more active phase of reflecting on what they have heard and seen in the next step.

Step 4: First Centering Prayer Period

I outlined the practice of centering prayer in the last chapter, but let me briefly reiterate the basic structure of this practice before explicitly considering its adaptation for mystical reflection. In its most basic form, centering prayer is just three things: sitting quietly with your eyes closed, a chosen word as a mental focus, and a designated amount of time set aside for the practice. When I facilitate regular weekly group meetings, or teach the practice in a weekend workshop on centering prayer, I adhere to the full method and time recommendation of twenty minutes. The centering prayer periods in mystical reflection are somewhat truncated; however, this first centering prayer period most closely resembles the traditional format developed by Thomas Keating and M. Basil Pennington.[5] There are only a few tweaks at this juncture, and they should be open for experimentation and customization according to the needs of the group.

First, one of the major issues which facilitators should pay special attention to is creating the right amount of silence and solitude for this period. In a home setting, this necessity may be more difficult than it first appears. A certain amount of silence may

---

4. And, contact me about what you try and what works! I'm intensely curious to know the variety of experiences and ways to communicate those experiences.

5. Pennington, *Centering Prayer*, xv–xvii.

The Method of Mystical Reflection

not mean complete and total silence for your group. With groups that I have led, I offer the possibility of playing some meditative music quietly during these times. These groups have universally declined any musical accompaniment, but see what works best for your group. While some amount of noise may be unavoidable, the group needs to decide what to do about children, pets, and any sources of possible interruption.

In groups which I have facilitated, the child issue is typically the most significant one. With older children, it may be possible to "strike a deal" for assistance in creating times of silence. This tactic is typically less effective with younger children. With the younger set, it may be worthwhile to find some means of childcare where the kids are not in the room and maybe not even in the house. Perhaps you could try having childcare at another location. Of course, that raises the issue of who will be supervising the children. As you can see, multiple factors go into creating even a temporarily silent environment. Also, you may never be able to guarantee a time that is completely without distraction. If so, just proceed as best you can, and try to find your own balance.

Third, you will want to agree on a set time limit for the centering prayer periods. The amount of time really depends on the consensus of the group. If there are few time constraints on the group, you may desire a full twenty-minute period; although, remember that mystical reflection has two centering prayer periods, so plan accordingly. You'll need to find a middle ground that works for the entire group. In my initial groups, I used only five-minute periods. Now, some of the participants, including me, had practiced centering prayer and/or meditation for years. Five minutes seemed quite short to us. However, to other members, five minutes seemed a stretch at first. Eventually, five minutes came to be a time for all of us to pause and settle but still feel like we could have gone longer once the time was over. That's a good balance. Mystical reflection is not about stretching anyone to the point of discomfort. Also, I recommend using a designated timer with a gentle sound when the time has elapsed. Many good apps are available to set up a phone for this type of use. I do discourage use of any alarm that includes a jarring sound. It might be great to wake you up in the morning, but it can really disorient someone emerging from centering prayer. Time constraints should be chosen to enhance, not detract from, the overall experience.

Aside from setting up a quiet environment and designated time period, there is not any necessary difference between this first centering prayer period and the traditional format of the practice. I do not even recommend deviating from your typical chosen sacred word, if you practice centering prayer on your own. If you do not already center at other times, please feel free to center with any word that will gently remind you of your intention to wait for God in prayer. The word might be *God, love, hope*, or any other word that reminds you of why you are sitting still whenever your mind wanders off for a moment. The second centering prayer period will partake more completely of the content and context of mystical reflection, but this first period is useful to settle and calm yourself with the details of the meeting's ME still ringing in your ears. Once the group is centered after this fashion, they are ready to hear the account of the ME anew, perhaps now with the ears of spiritual listening a bit more open.

Step 5: Second Telling/Reading of a Mystical Experience (ME)

In this step, we have reached the heart of mystical reflection because participants will now begin to focus actively on reflecting. Each member of the group has now had ample time to settle and center, hear the ME, and move into a focus on that experience while the frenetic static of everyday life has receded into the background. During the first telling/reading of an ME, group participants were relatively passive listeners, but in the second telling/reading they will move into a more active phase. At this point, the facilitator should provide all members of the group with something on which to write along with a writing utensil. For each participant, I recommend giving your total attention to the sharer's story. Listen for any word or phrase that stands out to you—that

The Method of Mystical Reflection

"shimmers"—even if it seems to be subsidiary, inconsequential, or tangential to the point of the ME. Also, be aware of any images that might rise up in your mind in connection with the telling of the ME. Write down any notes that will remind you of that word, phrase, image, or even feeling that stands out to you. You might even write down several possibilities at this point. In a later stage, you'll choose one to focus on, but you don't need to worry about that right now. See the following examples of note cards that I wrote during second tellings/readings of mystical reflection groups. I have circled the word/phrase/image that I eventually used for the next stage of mystical reflection.

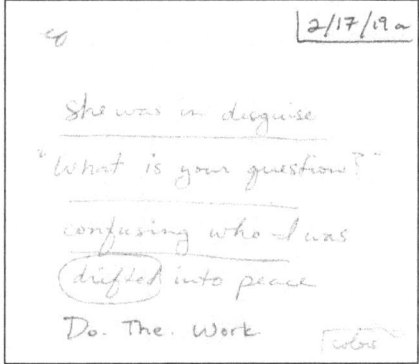

Figure 1

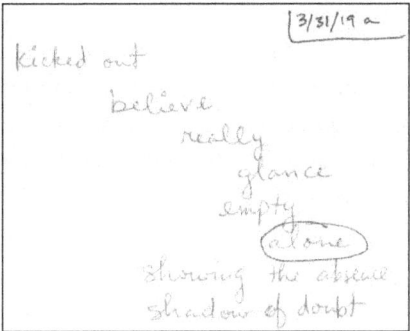

Figure 2

In case my writing is difficult to interpret, I circled the word *drifted* in figure 1 and the word *alone* in figure 2. While I am offering some examples here, please don't be bound to follow my pattern. Write down whatever stands out to you, and arrange your notes however you want. The point is to provide something to aid your memory for the next stage of mystical reflection (and potentially create a reminder to use in the coming days as you go back into your everyday life).

Before proceeding on to the next step, I want to emphasize two important factors in the active listening which groups will engage in here. Facilitators will need to be scrupulously conscious of these pieces in particular. First, you are not—I repeat, NOT—trying to interpret the ME for the person who experienced it. While that person has relayed the story of the ME to everyone in the group, the personal interpretation of that experience for him/her is unique to her/him. Perhaps that person may desire to seek out one-on-one spiritual direction to aid in his/her interpretation, but that is not the purpose of a mystical reflection group. Mystical reflection is an opportunity for the experience *itself*, not its interpretation, to impact the members of the group. In groups that I have facilitated, it was exceedingly common that what stood out to group members was completely different from what the experience meant to the sharer.[6] This is one of the few particularities of the method that took some time for groups to understand. As facilitator, I did gently remind participants from time to time to veer back into statements of personal reflection and away from "impartial" interpretation for the person who experienced the ME.

Second, I want to stress that there is nothing wrong if no word, phrase, or image stands out to you during the tellings/readings of the ME. Similarly to *lectio Divina*, centering prayer, and a host of other Christian spiritual practices, the point of a spiritual practice is not to receive an insight, experience, or even a devotional thought every single time. I encourage you to be open to the negative experience in mystical reflection as well. Sometimes, we just don't "get" anything. Methods work all the time with science

---

6. While the sharer may indeed receive a new insight about his or her own experience through what others eventually share, each group member is making a statement of how the *story* impacted him or her, not the ME itself.

and machines. Mystical reflection is not a method in that sense, and it is based on the personal interaction of a relationship both in terms of group participants with each other and between each participant and the divine. That's a messy place; it won't always "work." As a result, I cannot overstress the necessity to give yourself space and permission to feel or hear nothing at all. That doesn't mean you've failed because you have still been an active participant in holding the space with a person who has shared a very intimate experience of their lives with you. That is a deep and spiritual act in and of itself.

At other times, something may stand out to you, and you don't have a clue as to why. That's okay. In fact, that's wonderful! Take that image, word, or phrase, and ponder on it—treasure it in your heart[7]—after the mystical reflection group meeting time. You never know when the time will be right for that reflection to break into your own experience. Still, whether something stands out to you or not, a later step of mystical reflection offers an opportunity to share that piece with the other group members. Remember, as we transition to the next few steps, along with this one, we are entering a deeply intimate place for group members. Sharing occurs best when people feel that they can let their guard down, so it is vital to maintain the safe-space atmosphere which has been created by the previous steps and environmental conditions.

Step 6: Second Centering Prayer Period

After the second telling/reading, the group enters a second period of centering prayer. In many ways this time will echo the earlier period in terms of length of time, silence, and location; but there are a couple of important differences in this second opportunity for centering prayer. First and foremost, the sacred word used to focus will shift. Instead of your usual word, substitute the word, phrase, or image that stood out to you during the ME tellings/readings. Now perhaps multiple words stood out to you. As you

---

7. Luke 2:19.

can see from my note card examples above, that was often my personal experience. There isn't one right way to choose which word, phrase, or image to use in centering prayer. Maybe one word stands out above all the others. If so, try using that one. If one aspect of the ME does not stand out more than others, just begin by choosing one at random. In my experience, I often discovered that such a random choice was not as random as I thought at first. Also, I, and others in groups which I have facilitated, have had centering experiences in which I began to center with one word or phrase, and another one simply pushed it out of my consciousness. My advice is not to fight such a shift. Allow it to happen and sit with the new word, phrase, or image. It might be a valuable reflection in and of itself to consider why one word pushed out the other. Even as you remain open concerning word usage, you will also want to be open concerning the overall experience of this second centering prayer period.

Another important difference, which may sound a bit counterintuitive, is not to expect any specific experience or result from the word, phrase, or image. Now, there isn't anything wrong with having a particular feeling or experience arising out of this centering prayer period. The wrinkle lies in the word *expect*. While mystical reflection is a method to help one make sense of MEs, one of the most consistent and noticeable features of touching the ethereal plane is that the divine simply won't be bound to schedules. As you likely have noticed previously in this book, or in my earlier book *Just Begin*, I do not advocate any spiritual activity that will supposedly *induce* an ME. Whether mystical practices or mystical experiences, I am talking about what one can do *after* an ME has occurred in order to integrate the experience into his/her spirituality, both individually and communally. As a result, during this second centering prayer period, I encourage an attitude of "choiceless awareness."[8] In other words, if something happens or stands out to you as you pray, then great. If nothing stands out to

---

8. Kabat-Zinn, *Full Catastrophe Living*, 69. Kabat-Zinn defines *choiceless awareness* as "simply being present with and receptive to whatever unfolds in each moment as you rest in awareness."

The Method of Mystical Reflection

you at all, that's also great. Mystical reflection is designed to help people integrate MEs into their communal and individual spirituality, but that does not mean that you are producing anything. *Success* is defined in mystical reflection in the sense of community acceptance and well-being, coupled with an experiential realization that *God speaks*; success is not tied to any particular experience, insight, or enlightenment. This nonproductive attitude is essential to hold onto as you and your group enter into the next stage in which group members share their perceptions.

Step 7: Sharing Time

Allow me for a moment to digress from a description of this step to note that I almost left this step out, and I remain ambivalent about it. Mystical reflection, like ME itself, is not a recipe in order to get an instant result. The reflection aspect of mystical reflection is not meant to be limited to the space of an hour or two during which the group meets. While the communal sharing aspects of mystical reflection may be limited to the group meeting, recurring reflection is intended to last throughout the coming week or weeks until the group meets again. The new word, phrase, or image that you centered with during the last step can now become the sacred word you use in centering prayer or other devotional periods until the group meets again. Perhaps no new insights occur between meetings, but that is the natural place that they are located—*between* meetings. I do recommend a stage in which participants can share any immediate impressions they have had during the tellings/readings of the ME and subsequent centering prayer periods as long as groups remember that immediate impressions are not supposed to be the *only* impressions.

In this sharing time, the group can see to what extent the ME has *directly* affected their spiritual perspectives rather than only *indirectly* through the mediated interpretation of the ME. Group members may share any insights that they have had during the meeting. Find the right flow for your group, but I usually just ask for a volunteer to go first. We then proceed as each person desires to say something, but no one is required to share. The only major recommendation that I have here is that the sharer go last of all. He/she has had the longest time to sit with his/her own experience. It is at this juncture that the sharer can tell exactly what the ME means to him or her. In their earlier tellings/readings, they should be focused on the events of the experience itself with interpretive comments kept to a minimum. This order of sharing has been extremely fruitful in groups which I have facilitated because it allowed the sharer to see how the events of the ME affects/influences other members of the group without any of the personal context that was likely integral in the understanding of the person who actually experienced the ME. Also, sharers were often pleasantly surprised because what people chose to focus on often allowed them to see their ME from a new perspective. Now, for each sharer, it might feel a little awkward to relate an ME without their interpretation, especially if they feel quite strongly about its meaning. I encourage you to endure this discomfort because there are many opportunities in spiritual communities for the *interpretation* of various religious experiences to impact those who haven't had them. The intention of mystical reflection is to provide one method that an ME could *directly* impact other persons in your spiritual community without the intermediating factor of personal interpretation.

While most of my directive recommendations concern speaking order and how the sharer should proceed, it is also vital for other group members to follow some instructive norms in the process of mystical reflection. Many of these norms will be considered in the next chapter, but a few of them are so vital to the method that they cannot wait to be treated later. First, remember that the sharer of the ME is *always* sharing something that is very intimate and personal to them. Often it will be something that they are in some measure afraid to share with others. Be sensitive to that situation. Through that sensitivity, next, I urge all group members in the most strident terms that I can imagine: do NOT interpret the ME for the sharer. You are not telling them what the experience objectively means or what it means to them (i.e., the

The Method of Mystical Reflection

sharer). You are saying what stood out to you ONLY. Also, bear in mind that you are only speaking about your first impression. As you sit with this experience over the coming days or weeks, it is particularly likely that you will gain more insight yourself. Keep these directives in mind, and your group should be able to flow smoothly through this sharing time and be enriched by all the differing spiritual perspectives brought to the unique moment of sharing the story of this ME together. From the strength of this shared moment, participants may proceed to the final step of the method: prayer and parting.

Step 8: Ending Prayer for Guidance and Parting

While the sharing time as outlined above may naturally seem like a good ending stage for the mystical reflection method, this final step should not be overlooked because it is simple. In many ways, this ending step is about coming back up from the spiritual depths. First, an ending prayer for guidance helps to seal the time together as a discrete practice. In so doing, you may experiment with using a fixed prayer. For instance, you could use this one from the *Book of Common Prayer*:

> O God, by whom the meek are guided in judgment, and light *riseth* up in darkness for the godly: Grant us, in all our doubts and uncertainties, the grace to ask what *thou wouldest* have us to do, that the Spirit of wisdom may save us from all false choices, and that in *thy* light we may see light, and in *thy* straight path may not stumble; through Jesus Christ our Lord. Amen.[9]

While a fixed prayer may work in the beginning, I have found that as group members get to know each better that it is particularly appreciated if a volunteer prays extemporaneously for the sharer and for all to continue in the reflection which we have all begun together.

9. Howe, *Book of Common Prayer*, 832; italics in original. As I mentioned in my previous quotation of the *BCP*, I like to update the italicized words with their modern variants.

Following this prayer, the group can shift focus back to the general flow of life while remembering to carry their mystical reflections with them until they meet again. The rest of the meeting time can wind down with some light conversation, plans for next time, or even dessert if your group has incorporated sharing a meal with the conversational aspects of mystical reflection. However, I want to reemphasize that mystical reflection is not intended to be done at this point. Carry that reflection forward throughout the days or weeks until your group meets again. Additional insights may occur to you in this manner, but there are two other common outcomes that I have noticed in groups which I have facilitated. First, keeping a reflective attitude at the forefront of your mind connected to the shared ME helps to open your eyes to the small, little "coincidences" of life that could easily be seen as mystical. If we are not looking for such coincidences, then they so often just pass by us completely unnoticed, like an unheard whisper. Second—and this outcome completely floored me—participants occasionally had MEs that incorporated some of the content of the MEs shared during mystical reflection. In other words, the spiritual practice of mystical reflection on a past ME occasionally directly affected the spirituality of others in the group through instigating *new* MEs. It wasn't uniform, and it definitely wasn't predictable, but it happened nonetheless. Carrying the reflection into everyday life has direct, and sometimes quite striking, effects.

Any new experiences can also be shared with your group through various avenues. Please feel free to experiment with the best way to do that type of sharing. I have not found an ideal way to do so in my own experience. One avenue I have tried has been to set up social media groups in order to facilitate sharing in between meetings. Social media can be helpful to record the immediacy of impact on one's life by mystical reflection in the daily press of life. Also, it can pay that impact forward by reminding others in the group of the previous meeting and its content. While I thought that idea would be particularly contagious, I found use of these groups to be rather spotty and inconsistent. Often, these social media groups devolved into quick ways to remind the group

The Method of Mystical Reflection

when and where to meet. Another way to share, as noted above, is to incorporate these reflections from in between mystical reflections into the check-in period of the next meeting. This option provides more structure to sharing how the mystical reflection impacted members in between meetings, but this type of sharing could easily expand the time needed for check-in to the point of extensively lengthening the entire group meeting time. If any group members have an issue with time restrictions for meeting, then this option may not be viable. In light of these inconsistent results, try one of these options, or both, see if they work for you, and experiment with anything that might work better for your specific group. Remember that mystical reflection is an open-ended and organic method that allows a lot of flexibility for customization and change. It has to be open because MEs just don't fit themselves into nice and neat boxes. As a result, any reflective process that takes MEs seriously must be equally adaptive.

Okay, that's it. Those are the pieces to the method. Go try it out! In the rest of this book, I offer some important tips for facilitators, expanded descriptions of mystical reflection meetings I have facilitated for all of you who want specific examples (chapter 5), and many historical MEs (chapter 6) that your group may decide to use for reflection, either as you first begin to meet or when you have a meeting in which the sharer does not wish to share any personal ME of his/her own. These pieces are important to put flesh on the bones of the method in this chapter, but you can begin using it right now. I am definitely the kind of person that wants a few simple instructions before being let go to play with finding my own way. Please feel free to join me in this approach. If you are the type of person that wants a more complete picture, then that's great too; you can adventure on into the next several chapters to get all the details. Either way, let's get reflective!

CHAPTER 5

Group Dynamics

With the method of mystical reflection introduced, you can jump right into practice; however, there are many logistical issues in setting up a small group, particularly a small group dealing with such a unique type of experience. In the vein of practical necessity, this chapter is a resource for anyone setting up a new mystical reflection group or fine-tuning an existing group. With this focus, I want to proceed with issues in the order they arose in the groups which I have facilitated, so we will begin with the basics of setting up the group and the expectations you and the participants may have going into this new space. Following basic setup, I want to offer sections that are more specifically geared to the needs of facilitators and participants, respectively. We'll draw this chapter to a close with two narratives of a group mystical reflection so you can see examples of all the pieces moving together. Now, doubtless your group will have its own idiosyncrasies, so please don't try to reproduce exactly what you see in those narratives. Look at the information in this chapter as loose guidelines to assist you in finding what works best, knowing that "best" will look different for every group.

Setting Up the Group

When you are first forming a group, there are many options for customization and exploration, but there are a few points where you may need to make a firm decision from the outset. Typically, firm decisions surround logistical matters. For instance, you'll need to ask and answer some questions of structure. Where will you meet? In homes? At church? Will you vary your meeting space on a rotation? How often will you meet? During what time of day will you meet? How frequently will your group meet? Will the responsibilities of facilitator be on one person, or will they be passed around to everyone in the group? There are no objectively right answers to these questions, but there are better and worse answers to these questions for your particular group. Also, don't be afraid to try something out for a trial period and decide whether it works or not. You don't need to keep any specific piece; however, as you may suppose from this type of scenario, I recommend setting up some method for ongoing evaluation of the group among its members. This evaluation does not have to happen at every meeting, but it likely would be helpful to evaluate every few months or so. One last firm decision for group setup should center on the role of silence and mystery in the group. As is true for groups that form on the basis of more general spiritual direction,[1] mystical reflection groups are dealing with a great mystery through experience and the telling of experiences. Silence is the natural language for mystery, and, as a result, silence should have a place in your group. Don't rush too quickly to find answers. Be willing to sit in silence, to stretch out those moments, and feel the discomfort of not knowing. While several aspects of setting up a group require firm, practical decisions, the utility of silence in group meetings is to remind everyone that practical logistics only go so far when dealing with MEs. Similarly, group setup should treat to one degree or another the thorny issue of expectations.

What do you expect from group mystical reflection? What does "success" look like? It is tempting to leap to the conclusion

---

1. Dougherty, *Group Spiritual Direction*, 35.

that you are all gathered together in order to agree on an interpretation concerning the meaning of an individual ME. Trust me, you'll only need to meet a time or two to find out that agreeing by consensus on the meaning of an ME is a very rare happening. However, if you can't focus on the interpretation of experiences as a measure of success, then what do you measure, particularly if you have periodic evaluations of the group? Perhaps a story will help a bit to explore this conundrum:

> The students asked the master, "What is spirituality?" He said, "Spirituality is that which succeeds in bringing one to inner transformation." The students then asked, "But if I apply the traditional methods handed down by the masters, is that not spirituality?" The master answered, "It is not spirituality if it does not perform its function for you. A blanket is no longer a blanket if it does not keep you warm, so spirituality does change. People change. Needs change. What was spirituality once is spirituality no more. What generally goes under the name of spirituality is merely the record of past methods."[2]

In other words, there are no quick and easy answers about what constitutes a "successful" ME, and our expectations for what constitutes a "successful" mystical reflection should reflect that reality. Does that mean that there are no ways to tell if growth is happening? No, I don't think so, but we do need to change how we think and what we expect in order to see growth.

As you are setting up, joining, or maintaining your group, keep in mind three forms of expectation that can help you assess the health of the group. First, as you pay attention to the MEs that individuals relate, are you able to see where God has been? This standard of expectation for ME is well established, reaching all the way back to Moses himself.[3] When Moses asks to see God, God does not let Moses see his face. That would be too much for Moses; rather, God allows Moses to see his back. Metaphorically, this tale reminds us that we are able to see where God has been far

---

2. De Mello, *Song of the Bird*, 11.
3. Exod 33:18–23.

better than where he is. Start there. This perspective emphasizes the direction of mystical reflection. Specifically, mystical reflection is concerned with MEs that have happened, not in inducing MEs in the present. If an ME occurs within a mystical reflection, or as the result of a mystical reflection, then celebrate that occurrence, but do not expect it as a guaranteed result of the method. Second, the measure of expectation for your group can be seen through the support each participant gives to each other when life is difficult. After all, MEs are not the only part of the spiritual life. Quantitatively speaking, the times of the "dark night of the soul"[4] are far more frequent than the brief contemplative moments. Are the participants in the group walking together through these tough times? If so, that's a healthy group. A final area to relocate expectations for the group is in all participants coming to expect God to be found in surprising, often ordinary, places. This expectation developed in the groups I facilitated, and it is always my favorite part to see. It's amazing how much we see once we begin to look for something. One of my group participants noted how the group had opened her eyes to the closeness of ME through these words: "It also struck me that we seek out books where we can read about the mystical experiences of famous people but we don't ask the people closest to us about their experiences." I couldn't say it better myself. By shifting our expectations, we're learning a new way to see. However, new ways of seeing do not begin by magic; they begin with conscious intention and attention, particularly on the part of the facilitator(s).

Facilitators

Before diving into expectations and responsibilities for facilitators, we honestly could start with the question, "Does a group need a facilitator?" While there is a lot of room for adaptation and

---

4. This term refers to an expansive mystical tradition beginning with St. John of the Cross (Juan de la Cruz). See as a representative example, John of the Cross, *Selected Writings*, 155–210. See more specifically in terms of a group context Hopcke, "Spiritual Direction and Mystical Experience," 86–88.

customization, there does need to be someone to help the group move along the steps of the mystical reflection process. Of course, that doesn't always have to be the same person, and/or a group could divvy up tasks among multiple people. Still, I want to proceed here on the basis of having a set facilitator at least for the purposes of discussion. In that light, let's move deeper through the question, "What is expected of a facilitator?" We can best dig into that question by looking at what a facilitator is not and what a facilitator is.

Being a facilitator for a mystical reflection group is *not* about being a specific type of person. For instance, a mystical reflection facilitator does not need to be a trained therapist or counselor but should be ready to refer a person to a trained professional if the need arises. A mystical reflection facilitator does not need to have lots of overt mystical experiences him- or herself. Also, unlike with group spiritual direction, the mystical reflection facilitator does not necessarily need a background as a spiritual director.[5] A mystical reflection facilitator does not even need to be a person who has an ongoing one-on-one relationship with a spiritual director, although it definitely could enhance anyone's life to have such a one-on-one relationship.[6] Basically, a facilitator does not need to have any special abilities or training; rather, she or he needs to be committed to doing a certain set of tasks.

For facilitators, what needs to be done begins with tasks on an attitudinal level. On the attitudinal level, mystical reflection facilitators need to commit to the uncomfortable place of powerlessness, of being nondirective.[7] It is not the job of the facilitator to make a group look like a textbook example of one of the narrative sessions presented later in this chapter. Each group will be different; each group will need to evolve to find its place. A mystical reflection facilitator should not force the group into a mold but recognize the shape that the group is taking as it develops. Within the context of the meeting session, the facilitator will also need to

5. Fryling, *Seeking God Together*, 27–28.
6. Fryling, *Seeking God Together*, 121.
7. Guenther, *Holy Listening*, 94.

model an active listening mode. For instance, speaking directly to facilitators here: frame questions as restatements of what a participant is sharing, share what you are hearing them say, ask for clarification, and offer connections from other sessions or previous participant MEs. Conversely, always be ready to say nothing at all, if that's what the group needs. Remember that, above all, the job of the mystical reflection facilitator is to help the group listen to the Holy Spirit.[8] The facilitator's job is not to "conjure up" the Holy Spirit; rather, the primary job is to minimize distractions. That aim comes far more from attitude than action, so cultivate the attitudes noted above. In addition, there are some specific actions that a facilitator needs to perform for the group, beginning with ensuring a safe space for those who are sharing an ME.

The first and foremost active task for the mystical reflection facilitator is to ensure that the group is a safe space to share the reading or telling of an ME. If people don't feel free to share, then there isn't much point in going any further. While all persons have a responsibility to uphold group norms, which will be presented in a later section, the facilitator has the added responsibility of protecting and reminding the group concerning the absolute confidentiality of all that is said within it.[9] Additionally, facilitators should foster an attitude of acceptance among group participants. Acceptance means creating an atmosphere that is open, not judgmental, in order to "welcome whatever part of the soul chooses to reveal itself. We welcome it in love."[10] Don't lose sight that the mystical reflection group is all about *listening* not interpreting or directing. The group needs to be a safe space for participants to listen to others and feel that they are heard. In fact, the necessity of a safe space is so important that I recommend taking the first meeting or two to go over guidelines, norms, and expectations at length. Perhaps these logistical meetings might even need to be followed for another session or two of working with historical MEs

8. Fryling, *Seeking God Together*, 43.

9. Absolute confidentiality barring, of course, any communication that would necessitate contacting professional help or the authorities.

10. Fryling, *Seeking God Together*, 21.

that did not happen to the participants themselves. If you wish this type of measured introduction for your group, you can turn to the next chapter for many accounts of MEs in history. No matter how you slice it, the first major action for a mystical reflection facilitator is to ensure a safe space for the intentional sharing of sensitive subjects.

Secondly, facilitators do their most obvious work of facilitation when helping discussion flow smoothly in the group mystical reflection session. While the previous tasks, attitudinal and active, may not be obvious, this task will be front and center in almost every mystical reflection session. Active listening skills will come in very handy at this point. Facilitators will likely be dealing with multiple levels of language and multiple levels of interpretation. After all, MEs tend to move back and forth between the mundane "water" and the highly symbolic and metaphorical "living water" levels of language.[11] Facilitators don't need to be perfect in navigating connections between these levels of communication, but facilitators need to realize that these issues will appear time and time again.

Navigating discussion flow is easier to recognize in some specific examples rather than simply through general principles. For instance, it often happens that one or two members of the group will tend to be extra talkative or have a tendency to have action-packed weeks when check-in time rolls around. In order to avoid the dominance of particular persons during this time or to avoid check-in stretching out in length to impact negatively the meat of mystical reflection, one might introduce an analogy or metaphor to create some distance for persons from their own experience. For example, you might ask everyone "If your past week were a box lunch, then what would have been in it?" It is often easier to curtail overly chatty persons in this way since they likely couldn't fit a five-course meal in a lunch box. This analogical piece can also be helpful to draw out the more reticent members of the group. Participants who had a bad week might not need to say so; rather, he they could simply say that they felt like they had a "banana"

11. John 4:1–26.

Group Dynamics

of a week where they "slipped on the peel." Imagery of this sort also serves as a bridge from lighthearted small talk to the deeper subjects that will often present themselves as a person shares an ME of his or her own. As a second discussion flow example, sometimes an individual has an ME happen to them, and they simply can't wait to share that with everyone. Of course, if that is the case, the person who is next up in any previously agreed upon rotation schedule should be consulted and respected with whether to allow that other person to cut in line or not. One disclaimer which I would like to offer particularly for facilitators is to be on the watch for the type of participant that has many MEs and wants to share immediately and often. You don't want other group members to feel pushed to the side or overwhelmed by such a large personality. Examples illustrating the necessity for facilitators to manage discussion flow could easily proliferate beyond these two, but they offer an idea of what to look for when paying attention to discussion flow.

At the very least, facilitating discussion flow will require the constant reminder on the part of the facilitator that there is no one right answer or interpretation. Varying aspects of an ME will stand out to different people. That's really the fun of Step 7: Sharing Time. It's amazing how different the perspectives can be. Just remember that no one is interpreting the ME *for* the one who is sharing. It is all about how the telling or reading of that event impacts those who hear it. Mystical reflection is not about solving problems—except for the problem of listening and feeling listened to. That's where the facilitator needs to focus the magic of the method: listening. Additionally, that constant reminder need not be heavy-handed or overly serious. Use humor and lightheartedness whenever possible. It has the benefit of reminding the facilitator him- or herself that she or he is not responsible for getting the "right" interpretation. In fact, humor itself has the potential for mystical experience.[12] Whether by humor or not, facilitators are most visibly facilitating when attending to the flow of

12. Hair, "Three Basic Questions," 70–71.

discussion, and that aspect should be one of the topics for ongoing group evaluation.

Group evaluation is important to consider on its own because it is not only an activity that the facilitator needs to promote, but it is also an activity in which the facilitator should take a back seat. The frequency of group evaluation can range widely depending on the needs and desires of your group from every few weeks up to once every two or three months. I do recommend evaluation once every three months at the very least. Concerning questions, there are no questions that are completely required, but if you would like a place to start, then you can use some questions that crop up often in the practice of group spiritual direction. For instance, you might ask:

> How prayerful were we during this session [or week, month, or quarter]? What was the quality of our silence? Our attention to God? What seemed to take us from attention to God? How well did we stay focused on the spiritual life of each person, on the God relationship beneath the content of what people presented? Where did we get off course? Were there places where we got "off track" (e.g., doing too much problem solving, being too analytical or philosophical, sharing our own experiences during another's time when it wasn't called for)?[13]

Also, group evaluation is a time for participants to evaluate the methods and quality of facilitation, so facilitators might expect the need to build some critical distance for themselves. Participant comments on the facilitation process are not necessarily comments about the facilitator as a person, and they definitely do not reflect on their *worth* as persons. Evaluation is all about making the group as effective as possible, meaning that all grow spiritually. It is a time for each person to look within and consider how he or she may have grown over the past weeks or months. Each person will then need to weigh for her- or himself as to what changes should be made on a personal and communal level. The facilitator's job in group evaluation is to help the group steer a balanced

---

13. Dougherty, *Group Spiritual Direction*, 54.

course that allows for safety and comfort to share, along with the sober honesty that leads to growth.

Looking back, the foregoing tasks may sound difficult when laid out one right after another, but each task tends to support and blend in with the others as one gets familiar with the role of facilitator. Facilitating a group through mystical reflection does not require any great degree of prior knowledge or experience. It does require a commitment to one's own attitude and spirituality, as well as a commitment to the group tasks of creating a safe space, shepherding the flow of discussions, and ensuring regular group evaluation. These responsibilities may sound quite weighty, but facilitators are not working alone or in a vacuum. Each and every participant has obligations for the cohesion of the group. All participants have a part to play in mystical reflection.

Participants

While setting up the group may be a responsibility for the facilitator(s), participants have contributive responsibilities as well, and two of these responsibilities deserve particular attention. First, all participants have a responsibility to be active listeners. Active listening is needed to follow the steps of the method in noting words or phrases that stand out, but being an active listener is a more expansive role in mystical reflection. It is a major participant contribution toward the creation of a safe space that is sensitive to the needs of everyone in the group. In other words, participants should combine the traditional skills of active listening with some principles of respectful, compassionate communication to embody fully the role of active listener in the mystical reflection context. On the side of traditional active listening, participants need to remember the following steps:

* Through your posture and nonverbal behavior, you are showing the speaker whether you are paying attention. Face the speaker, make eye contact, make notes if necessary, and be present in body and mind to what is being said.

* Keep an open mind as the ME for the session is being shared, don't interrupt, and definitely don't attempt to "solve" the ME for the speaker.
* Listen to the telling, look for words and phrases that stand out, and try to picture what the speaker is saying.
* If you ask questions, make sure that they are asked only for the purpose of clarification.
* Be open to offering the speaker regular feedback. Nodding your head in agreement or simply saying "hmm" can go a lot farther than you think.
* Try to pay attention to what is not being said, to nonverbal cues.

These simple steps of active listening are front and center in mystical reflection sessions, but participants need to keep an eye on some additional, more comprehensive principles for creating an environment of mutual respect where honest communication is valued.

Principles of compassionate communication are not as easily reducible to bullet points as those for active listening, but they are nonnegotiable aspects that every participant needs to keep in mind within mystical reflection. First, as part of keeping an open mind, remember that it is okay to disagree on the meanings of MEs or particular parts of MEs. The mystical reflection group is not tasked with coming up with a consensus that fits all perspectives together logically. Mystical reflection is a place for both/and thinking, not either/or thinking. It's important simply to hear and value the differences of perspective. As the practical application of this principle, participants need to limit their comments to *I* statements: "I felt this way during the reading . . .," "This detail of the ME struck me in this way . . .," or "I was really drawn to this phrase . . ." Even if it seems more natural to speak in *you* statements about an experience you did not personally have, it is all too easy to come across as attacking or blaming someone who has shared a vulnerable piece of themselves. Second, as a participant, be aware

Group Dynamics

that people have different styles of communication. Some MEs will not be related in terms that make sense to you. In fact, the struggle of dealing with a story that is confusing to you can be your own focus for what stands out to you in an ME account. Additionally, this difficulty could open up a doorway for you to reexamine your own assumptions and preconceptions. It all reflects back on that attitude of open-mindedness. Third, the most important piece of compassionate communication in a mystical reflection group is the commitment to complete confidentiality. What is said in the group stays in the group. As each participant holds this trust for one another, it will become much easier to let your guard down in order to tell everyone about the MEs you have, whether seemingly ordinary or decidedly extraordinary. While this responsibility for compassionate, respectful communication and active listening is important to maintain on a personal level, it is also necessary for this responsibility to have a visible, preferably written, place within the norms of the mystical reflection group.

The second major responsibility that every participant in mystical reflection must face is the duty to uphold the stated group norms. It is an easy mistake to think that deciding and maintaining group norms is the responsibility of the facilitator, but everyone in the group shares responsibility for setting and keeping accountability for group norms. There are differing aspects to group norms, but these facets generally fall under formal group norms and informal standards that accrue in relation to the formal norms. Concerning formal group norms, consider adopting as a group something like the general respectful communication guidelines in the following acronym:

> R = take RESPONSIBILITY for what you say and feel without blaming others
> E = use EMPATHETIC listening
> S = be SENSITIVE to differences in communication styles
> P = PONDER what you hear and feel before you speak
> E = EXAMINE your own assumptions and perceptions

> C = keep CONFIDENTIALITY
>
> T = TRUST ambiguity because we are not here to debate who is right or wrong[14]

It is important to have formal, if generalized, guidelines for group norms, and I suggest having those guidelines verbally stated and visibly posted, at least as your mystical reflection group gets started. While formal norms should be in place from the outset, informal standards develop more slowly and intuitively over time.

I do not want to presume to tell you what the informal standards of your group should be, for those standards depend on the specifics of each individual group. However, I do want to share some of the informal standards that have arisen in conversations I have had with participants in mystical reflection groups that I have facilitated. In some ways, these standards reflected the formal norms, but they often veered off in directions that were important for the group. First, in connection with the formal norms, participants were concerned with creating and maintaining a safe space to hear and be heard. As part of that endeavor, they often focused on the necessity of sharing a meal which "increases the comfort level," as one participant put it, before any serious business gets underway. That initial comfort level grew over time as every member of the mystical reflection group worked hard to maintain an attitude of being "eager to hear others' stories," as another participant stated. As the central formal and informal standard, this atmosphere of "intimate vulnerability," in the words of one group member, took a high-profile place in group evaluations. Other informal standards were not as obviously connected to the formal group norms.

Informal standards tend to reflect each group idiosyncratically, so the following examples are not meant to be representative, merely illustrative. For example, the second most common informal standard to be noted in my groups was a recognition and sensitivity to the difficulty of describing or writing an ME. When looking forward to their turn as sharer, many participants became

---

14. Law, *Bush Was Blazing*, 86–87.

hyperaware of this issue. Third, and in part as a reaction to the difficulty of description, my groups tended to set silence as an informal standard. Of course, within the method of mystical reflection, there are particular times of silence built in, but participants also treated silence as a place to hold whenever one is not quite sure what an ME means to him or her or what stood out most in a telling. As a result, getting comfortable with silence became an informal standard through the practical repetitions of the method over the course of many group sessions. Finally, participants created an informal standard of widening their own sense of the range of mystical experience. One group member pithily stated during an evaluation period that this sense of range became "a way of claiming a true encounter with God" which she used to combat her natural tendency to discount her own experiences. This standard was also at work when participants pulled out of a reading or telling a detail which the sharer hadn't previously seen as significant. One way or the other, participants felt that this standard, in the language of one member, "helped further confirm the reality of the experience." All of these standards and norms in the last few pages, for both participants and facilitators, flow into a single experience for each session of group mystical reflection. Consequently, rather than offering more lists, let's draw this chapter on group dynamics to a close by seeing all of these logistical items working together in two accounts of actual mystical reflection sessions.

Two Narratives of Group Meeting

February 11, 2019

This meeting was quite early in the life of the particular mystical reflection group,[15] but it offers a typical example of how the ses-

---

15. This session was actually our first meeting to employ the method. The initial meeting was just an explanation of the method and logistical issues, such as setting up an order for sharers to proceed and divvying up responsibilities for meals and childcare. Transportation issues could also be considered at this juncture, but that was not a specific concern for this group.

sions would go. For scheduling reasons, we met in the evenings once every two weeks, usually from 7:00 p.m. to a little after 9:00 p.m. While this session had only four people, we later grew to include six to eight people who attended regularly. We always met in a home, and we met in the same home for the duration of this group. A comfortable and consistent setting helped to set everyone at ease. Additionally, while this specific group did not have childcare, we often had childcare provided for other groups through a paid sitter on site or at one of the other member's houses. For this session, we began to settle into the space with a home-cooked meal. The hosts provided the main dish for the meal, and all other participants contributed a side dish, salad, or dessert of some sort. As Step 1: Settling into the Space, we spent most of the first hour of this session eating, socializing, and generally catching up with each other, which was a time distribution pattern that became standard procedure. After that relatively lengthy period, and now with full bellies, we moved from the kitchen/dining area to the main room of the house in order to segue to the other steps of mystical reflection.

I guided the group into Step 2: Prayer for Guidance with a slightly modernized version of the prayer "For Guidance" from the *Book of Common Prayer*:[16]

> Direct us, O Lord, in all our doings with your most gracious favor, and further us with your continual help; that in all our works begun, continued, and ended in you, we may glorify your holy name, and finally, by your mercy, obtain everlasting life; through Jesus Christ our Lord. Amen.

Following this simple prayer, we moved to Step 3: First Telling/Reading of an ME. The sharer chose an ME which had actually happened to her, and she decided to read from a written account rather than proceeding extemporaneously. The following is her ME in her own words:

---

16. "For Guidance" (Prayer 57), in Howe, *Book of Common Prayer*, 832.

Group Dynamics

The dream began with me lying in bed. My bed was my childhood waterbed, and the bedroom was my childhood bedroom. The configuration of the room was from around the time I was ten years old. When I got up out of bed there were three other people in the bed as well, including two little girls (maybe twins) who were blond (like me) and overweight (like me) and a tall, skinny man with a mustache. I left the bedroom and went into my parent's living room. There were probably thirty or forty priests in the room, with albs and stoles on. I saw my spiritual director who is a priest as well as another priest in my diocese who was one of the people responsible for me becoming a priest. The stoles the priests had on were blue (for the season of Advent), but the stoles were special. The stoles had a Van Gogh "starry night" pattern on them. The stars swirled as I looked at them. My dad tapped me on the shoulder and asked me this question: "So, is this what you are going to be?" I said, "Yes." My spiritual director then said that it was time for all the priests to leave and to go sing "O Come, All Ye Faithful," like they do every year. They lined up and began leaving the house. I stood at the front door and held the door open for them as they left. As I walked out with them, I found myself across my hometown, standing on a corner of the road by the highway. There was a bus stop there, and I was sitting under an umbrella attached to a table waiting for the bus. All of a sudden, a dirty and disgusting man walked up to me. He was thin. His hair was long, greasy, and matted. It looked like he hadn't taken a shower for years, and he had a twin. The two walked almost as if they were slithering like snakes, and it was almost as if the two men were conjoined. One man talked the entire time while the other stayed silent. The man stood behind me and spoke into my ear. He said, "Where is she?" I answered, "Who?" The man said, "Where is your spiritual director? I am going to kill her." I got up in a panic, and I ran to a nearby restaurant to find her. She was sitting at a large, round table. Instead of directly talking to her, I talked to her husband, and I pleaded with him to get her to safety. The scene changed instantly, and my spiritual director and I were sitting on my childhood sofa, the sofa where I had endured so much abuse in real life. It is a sofa that appears in a lot of my dreams because so much psychological abuse happened there as a kid. The two disgusting men were back, and they had a gun pointed at my spiritual director's head. We were holding each other and crying. I was terrified, but I wouldn't let them kill her, so I placed my head between the gun and the head of my spiritual director. The next thing I knew, I was waking up on the sofa. The two men were gone. As I awoke, I saw my spiritual director standing in the hallway with one of the ten-year-old girls from the beginning of the dream. A light was shining on them. I got up, and I was naked, but I didn't care. I walked over to my spiritual director and she wrapped me in a white towel. She then took my face in her hands and said, "You have to remember. You have to know that you are filled with wine, oil, and an abundance of spices." She gave me a hug and then said that she had to put her granddaughter to bed.

While this ME was the account of a dream which occurred approximately three years prior to our session, the overall tenor of the reading was emotional and vulnerable. This mood was particularly apparent in the first reading.

After the first reading, we proceeded through Step 4: First Centering Prayer Period, Step 5: Second Telling/Reading of an ME, and Step 6: Second Centering Prayer Period with minimal comment. This flow among steps without specific opportunities for participants to speak was intentional on my part for two reasons. First, I wanted to aid the group in resisting the urge to comment on the ME account right away. As might be suspected, the shift in perspective from trying to interpret the ME account to simply recognizing what stood out to each person took every group a little time. Second, the movements among steps 3 through 6 are supposed to be reminiscent of waves gently lapping along the shore. Telling/reading, centering, telling/reading, centering, and so forth, allows the ME account to wash over all participants. The undulating action in these steps came to be the part which the majority of participants loved the most. Following the first centering prayer period, I handed out 3x5 index cards and pens, so everyone

Group Dynamics

could write down any words, phrases, or images that "shimmered" to them during the second reading of the ME account. Also, in this group, we kept the length of the centering prayer periods to five minutes. Each of those periods ended with a quiet tone on a phone that was set as the timer. From the back and forth of these middle steps, the group proceeded to talk about their initial reflections in Step 7: Sharing Time.

In sharing time, we transitioned from private, silent reflection to communal, shared reflection. We talked about our impressions, thoughts, and feelings surrounding the flow of the ME account and our experiences with it as the subject for centering. During sharing time, some participants referred to the notes they had made on index cards while others just spoke. We did not have an assigned order of sharing; each person just spoke when he or she felt ready. The only assigned portion for this step was to have the participant who experienced the ME go last. Each participant noted some aspect of word association in this sharing time. While most groups eventually moved to greater variety in reflective associations, it did seem that each group started with word association. For one participant, the word "spices" became the main semantic focus. For another, the focus centered on the words "vulnerable but determined" (which were not technically part of the reading). Following some initial comments on word association, one participant moved a bit further by noting that he found himself paying special attention to the various roles that clergypeople were filling in the dream. The sharer rounded out this time by noting that she felt drawn to meditate on the phrase "But if you can't," which was a phrase that had not previously occurred to her in connection with this memory.

After those final sharing comments, the group brought the formal mystical reflection to a close with Step 8: Ending Prayer for Guidance and Parting. We reread the Prayer of Guidance noted above; however, a different volunteer read the prayer. Following this close, I commented on my intention and desire for each of us to take that written word, phrase, or image to meditate on for the next two weeks. I informed the group that I had set up a private

Facebook group, so we could share our reflections and recollections throughout that time. Also, I reemphasized that we were not in the process of finding a "right" interpretation or coming to any type of consensus on the theological meaning of the ME; instead, I wanted us to keep in touch concerning how this mystical reflection continued to unfold in our lives in the coming days. After those brief comments, we all had dessert, which we had saved for after the "heavy lifting" of mystical reflection. We ended our evening in some additional light conversation to return to a more general level of consciousness after diving deep through group mystical reflection.

Interestingly, in the days and weeks that followed, multiple participants commented on the Facebook group that they had dreams in which a word, phrase, or image from the ME account "visited" them in their own dreams. In addition, one participant remarked on a change in perspective that specifically came from reflecting on the ME over time. She felt empowered to look more intentionally for the small spiritual moments in everyday life, moments that she once discounted as simple coincidence. For instance, a Scripture passage about "frankincense and myrrh" reminded her of the "spices" noted in the ME account. She could have easily brushed off that memory as inconsequential, but she was paying attention to small connections and the potential importance of them through the practice of mystical reflection.

March 3, 2019

The following account concerns a session with a different mystical reflection group which had been meeting together for a much longer period. As a result, while the basic pieces that are visible in the previous narrative are still there, this new example displays the potential of the mystical reflection process for modification and customization. As a group, we still met in the evening and shared a meal; however, we did incorporate childcare with this group because the group included seven adults along with three small children. We pooled our money to hire a sitter for the kids

Group Dynamics

in the group, and the sitter watched the kids next door while we conducted the mystical reflection session. We did have all of the children and the sitter there for the community meal. While of course this arrangement only worked the way it did because we happened to have two families living in close proximity, it is a great example of allowing your group to grow and change to fit your own situation. Following the time of eating and light conversation which constituted Step 1: Settling into the Space, we moved to the more overt steps of mystical reflection.

We segued physically from the kitchen/dining area to the main room of the house, and we segued mentally and spiritually with Step 2: Prayer for Guidance. We used the same prayer for this step that was quoted for the previous narrative account. At this point, we incorporated one significant difference from the previous narrative. Following the prayer, we had a short time for check-in during which each participant took about two minutes to tell the group about the past week. This check-in provided a necessary bridge between chatty and serious moods. Also, I introduced this period through a metaphor by asking the group, "If your week was a type of weather, then what would it be and why?" This group typically enjoyed the creative challenge of framing their week's events and their own feelings within the bounds of a metaphor. Answers included "partly cloudy," "bright and sunny," "gale force hurricane," and "constantly overcast and rainy." In all fairness, the entire previous week had actually been overcast and rainy fairly consistently. Still, this exercise helped us all to settle our focus in preparation for Step 3: First Telling/Reading of an ME.

The designated sharer of an ME for that night had written down his experience, and this is his account:

> As I stood waiting for the train to arrive that would take me from Bowie, Maryland, to Baltimore Penn Station, the gloominess of the day sank into my mind. I had recently run away from home because I was shunned by my mother for reasons of my identity. Mild relief came as the train approached the station. Immediately, as I entered the train it seemed as if the lights on the train

were dim and so was everyone else, except this man that was shining so bright I was attracted to sit next to him like a moth to a flame. I didn't really know why I sat next to him besides feeling a gentle, loving pull to do so. I sat next to him, and he radiated with such an intense glow that I started to feel warm. All of my suffering became quiet and faint, and I was filled with a sense of immense peace and love. The man turned and looked at me with bright brown eyes that were as bronze and shiny as his skin. He smiled at me, told me about a Bible study that happens via telephone and then handed me a green sticky note with the number of the Bible study. Then he said "Jesus loves you," which was also written on the sticky note. Upon hearing his voice my heart, mind, and soul pondered his words with great gratitude as tears of joy filled my eyes. We rode the train together in silence, and as we approached our stop we stood side by side waiting to exit. I felt as if I needed to thank him or at least to offer an Amen, but as soon as we stepped out of the doors of the train, I turned to my left, and he vanished.

Following that initial reading, we all entered Step 4: First Centering Prayer period. We then heard the story again in Step 5: Second Telling/Reading of an ME. Prior to this step, I had given everyone a pen and paper to write down anything that "shimmered" to them in the account. As this ME was written, the language and emotional tone of the account was roughly consistent between both readings, but it was only at this second reading that participants took notes. During the first reading, they simply listened to the story, so it could wash over them. We proceeded with Step 6: Second Centering Prayer period, using whatever word, phrase, or image stood out from that second reading.

As this group had been meeting for quite a while at this point, when we moved into Step 7: Sharing Time, comments ranged a bit further afield than word association, as seen in the previous narrative example. Multiple participants connected more to colors and images than words or phrases in this story; although, at least one participant did reflect directly on the phrase "Jesus loves you." Also, two participants connected this ME account to incidents in their

Group Dynamics

own personal past. As such, they offered their own interpretations of their past experiences in connection with this new ME story. I did interject at this point with a gentle reminder that we were not gathered to interpret the overall experience for the person who is sharing, and we were gathered to concentrate on only one experience at a time. At a later date, I had a personal conversation with the sharer for that evening, and I asked him whether he felt those comments were encroaching on his right to interpret for himself. He averred that they did not feel that way to him. Still, I want to caution each group to stay away from this line of comment when possible. Group comments concerning their own experiences also appeared in connection with the centering prayer periods. In fact, one participant noted that he started to use one word that stood out to him from the reading, *gratitude*, but the word *hope*, which was not part of the account, pushed it out as he prayed.

As you may be able to tell by comparing the two narratives, the differing perspectives of the sharing time grew the longer the groups met. This development displayed the health of the group and the deepening spiritual sensibilities of the participants as opposed to the aim of coming to a group consensus. The focus of sharing in each session was hearing all voices, not coming to some place of agreement. That was a vital piece for mystical reflection in practical application. Following sharing time, we moved to Step 8: Ending Prayer for Guidance and Parting. This group also customized mystical reflection at this point by incorporating a spontaneous prayer for the sharer and the entire group. Some groups chose to retain the prayer repetition in step 8; others desired to end extemporaneously. Either way works perfectly fine depending on the desires of the group. We all then embarked on the extended period of personal reflection as we parted ways for the week. However, before parting, this group savored ending the session with dessert, a customization favored by all groups although that may have had more to do with the quality of the cooking rather than the effectiveness of the method. Seriously though, while the role of meals in mystical reflection may seem silly, it is more important than it seems. As I have noted previously, sharing a meal is one of

Thinking Spiritually in Small Groups

the best ways to build community and a safe space among participants. Also, by having our meals in waves, we reinforced the sense of undulation that is also present in the back and forth of reading and centering prayer at the core of the method.

While these two narratives are unavoidably specific and idiosyncratic to these groups, I do hope that they serve to offer a window into seeing what the method of mystical reflection actually looks like in practice. This chapter has covered a lot of logistical ground. We started off with the expectations, parameters, and decisions that are necessary when a mystical reflection group first gets off the ground. These foundations were followed up by responsibilities and expectations for both facilitators and participants. Facilitators are tasked with ensuring the creation of a safe space, keeping the flow of discussion open and respectful, and guiding the entire group to periodic evaluations to guard against the group moving away from its purpose or toward any lack of regard for all its members. Participants also have commitments to live up to in mystical reflection. They are vitally involved with facilitators in creating and upholding group norms. Similarly, participants have the responsibility to listen to others actively and communicate respectfully before they ever get to the subject of any spiritual impact of the content. From all of these guidelines, it could be easy to come to the end of this chapter and feel weighed down with rules and regulations. It can be hard to remember that these are loose guidelines rather than rigid rules. Each group needs some answer to these issues, but they don't have to all look the same. For that reason, I wanted to offer a glimpse of a couple of sessions that have evolved in slightly different directions: mystical reflection in action. Most of the foregoing guidelines do not appear visibly in group meetings; they merely run along beneath the surface to make sure that all goes smoothly and that every viewpoint is valued. Your mystical reflection group does not need to look exactly like these, but I do hope the narratives give you some idea of where you are going. In that vein of thought, the next chapter provides many historical and personal ME accounts. One of the beautiful pieces of mystical reflection is that each participant can grow spiritually from an ME that he or she did not have personally. As a result, the experiences of the past hold just as much promise for spiritual growth as the events of the present.

CHAPTER 6

Examples of Mystical Experiences

Think of this final chapter as a reference tool. We have already gone over all the aspects of mystical reflection that you need to get started. After briefly introducing the reason for this method in the first chapter, we then proceeded in chapter 2 to defining the term *mystical experience* (ME) and the attendant spectrum along which MEs lie. Once the theoretical groundwork was in position, we looked at the mystical practices that form the foundation of mystical reflection—*lectio Divina* and centering prayer—in chapter 3, followed by the full explanation of the method in chapter 4. We rounded out the structure of mystical reflection in the fifth chapter with an investigation into group dynamics for facilitators and participants. Those are all the pieces you need to set up the group, but the beauty of mystical reflection is that anyone's ME can be the subject of a fruitful reflection.

In light of that wide range of possible mystical reflection application, the following ME accounts are provided. These accounts are especially helpful at the outset of a group. As you are creating a safe space, your group can practice the method without focusing on any one member of the group. Starting this way offers a little less pressure on those who are apprehensive about sharing. Additionally, your group can return to this chapter when no one has

Examples of Mystical Experiences

had a new experience on which the group wishes to reflect, or you can come here when the group wants to reflect on a certain type of ME. Consequently, whether your group is brand new or well established, this chapter on historical MEs has continuing utility for you.

In the following accounts, I have tried to collect a good cross-section of experiences. Many more examples of MEs could be included, but I have chosen these accounts to offer a sense of the breadth of the Mystical Spectrum. Also, I would encourage your group to investigate some of the books in my bibliography for additional ME accounts. The following accounts are grouped roughly in chronological order by major historical era. You will notice that I have included mostly Christian MEs, but I have thrown in a few from other religions. In your groups, I encourage all of you to try reflecting on some of these non-Christian pieces too. You might be surprised at what stands out to you. I am including a short index here at the beginning of the chapter to guide you to MEs of various specific types. Please note that the number in the index refers to my internal numbering system, *not* to page numbers. Now, let's reflect and have some fun!

Index

Auditory—4, 7, 9, 15, 20, 34, 54, 56
Centering Prayer—41, 42, 43, 45, 46, 47, 48, 49, 56
Communal Mystical Experience—8, 12, 14, 30
Conversion/Enlightenment—6, 9, 15, 22, 23, 30
Crying—39, 51
Divine Light—8, 9, 17, 29, 31, 32, 35, 36
Dream—1, 3, 10, 11, 54, 55
Labyrinth—49
Miracle—9, 12, 13, 14, 34
Music—35, 37
Nature—22, 25, 26, 28, 30, 40, 44, 48, 50
Oneness/Unity—27, 29, 32, 35, 37, 38, 42
Out of Body—35, 39

75

Thinking Spiritually in Small Groups

Physical Phenomena—2, 12, 13, 43
Poetry—5, 16, 18, 24
Sense of Presence—17, 23, 27, 33, 36, 39, 46, 51
Synchronicity/Coincidence—15, 44, 45, 47, 48
Vision (including "intellectual vision" or "imaginative vision")—4, 7, 8, 9, 10, 19, 20, 21, 29, 41, 46, 52, 53

Ancient Period (to AD 500)

Due to the age of these sources, these MEs tend to be located within the sacred writings of many different religions. There are many more examples within the scriptural traditions of the various world religions.

1. Jacob's Dream at Bethel[1]

Jacob left Beersheba and went toward Haran. He came to a certain place and stayed there for the night, because the sun had set. Taking one of the stones of the place, he put it under his head and lay down in that place. And he dreamed that there was a ladder set up on the earth, the top of it reaching to heaven; and the angels of God were ascending and descending on it. And the LORD stood beside him and said, "I am the LORD, the God of Abraham your father and the God of Isaac; the land on which you lie I will give to you and to your offspring; and your offspring shall be like the dust of the earth, and you shall spread abroad to the west and to the east and to the north and to the south; and all the families of the earth shall be blessed in you and in your offspring. Know that I am with you and will keep you wherever you go, and will bring you back to this land; for I will not leave you until I have done what I have promised you." Then Jacob woke from his sleep and said, "Surely the LORD is in this place—and I did not know it!" And he was afraid, and said, "How awesome is this place! This is none other than the house of God, and this is the gate of heaven." So Jacob rose

1. Gen 28:10–22 NRSV.

early in the morning, and he took the stone that he had put under his head and set it up for a pillar and poured oil on the top of it. He called that place Bethel; but the name of the city was Luz at the first. Then Jacob made a vow, saying, "If God will be with me, and will keep me in this way that I go, and will give me bread to eat and clothing to wear, so that I come again to my father's house in peace, then the LORD shall be my God, and this stone, which I have set up for a pillar, shall be God's house; and of all that you give me I will surely give one-tenth to you."

2. Jacob Wrestling an Angel[2]

The same night he got up and took his two wives, his two maids, and his eleven children, and crossed the ford of the Jabbok. He took them and sent them across the stream, and likewise everything that he had. Jacob was left alone; and a man wrestled with him until daybreak. When the man saw that he did not prevail against Jacob, he struck him on the hip socket; and Jacob's hip was put out of joint as he wrestled with him. Then he said, "Let me go, for the day is breaking." But Jacob said, "I will not let you go, unless you bless me." So he said to him, "What is your name?" And he said, "Jacob." Then the man said, "You shall no longer be called Jacob, but Israel, for you have striven with God and with humans, and have prevailed." Then Jacob asked him, "Please tell me your name." But he said, "Why is it that you ask my name?" And there he blessed him. So Jacob called the place Peniel, saying, "For I have seen God face to face, and yet my life is preserved." The sun rose upon him as he passed Peniel, limping because of his hip. Therefore to this day the Israelites do not eat the thigh muscle that is on the hip socket, because he struck Jacob on the hip socket at the thigh muscle.

---

2. Gen 32:22–32 NRSV.

3. Joseph's Dream[3]

Once Joseph had a dream, and when he told it to his brothers, they hated him even more. He said to them, "Listen to this dream that I dreamed. There we were, binding sheaves in the field. Suddenly my sheaf rose and stood upright; then your sheaves gathered around it, and bowed down to my sheaf." His brothers said to him, "Are you indeed to reign over us? Are you indeed to have dominion over us?" So they hated him even more because of his dreams and his words.

He had another dream, and told it to his brothers, saying, "Look, I have had another dream: the sun, the moon, and eleven stars were bowing down to me." But when he told it to his father and to his brothers, his father rebuked him, and said to him, "What kind of dream is this that you have had? Shall we indeed come, I and your mother and your brothers, and bow to the ground before you?" So his brothers were jealous of him, but his father kept the matter in mind.

4. Moses at the Burning Bush[4]

Moses was keeping the flock of his father-in-law Jethro, the priest of Midian; he led his flock beyond the wilderness, and came to Horeb, the mountain of God. There the angel of the Lord appeared to him in a flame of fire out of a bush; he looked, and the bush was blazing, yet it was not consumed. Then Moses said, "I must turn aside and look at this great sight, and see why the bush is not burned up." When the Lord saw that he had turned aside to see, God called to him out of the bush, "Moses, Moses!" And he said, "Here I am." Then he said, "Come no closer! Remove the sandals from your feet, for the place on which you are standing is holy ground." He said further, "I am the God of your father, the God of Abraham, the God of Isaac, and the God of Jacob." And Moses hid his face, for he was afraid to look at God.

3. Gen 37:5–11 NRSV.
4. Exod 3:1–15 NRSV.

5. Mystical Poetry: Hindu[5]

There the eye goes not;
Speech goes not, nor the mind.
We know not, we understand not
How one could teach it.
Other, indeed, is It above the known,
And moreover above the unknown.

6. The Enlightenment of Siddhartha Gautama (the Buddha)[6]

Siddhartha then made his way to a place near Bodh Gaya in India, where he found a suitable site for meditation. There he remained, emphasizing a meditation called "space-like concentration on the Dharmakaya" in which he focused single-pointedly on the ultimate nature of all phenomena. After training in this meditation for six years he realized that he was very close to attaining full enlightenment, and so he walked to Bodh Gaya where, on the full moon day of the fourth month of the lunar calendar, he seated himself beneath the Bodhi Tree in the meditation posture and vowed not to rise from meditation until he had attained perfect enlightenment. With this determination he entered the space-like concentration on the Dharmakaya. As dusk fell, Devaputra Mara, the chief of all the demons, or maras, in this world, tried to disturb Siddhartha's concentration by conjuring up many fearful apparitions. He manifested hosts of terrifying demons, some throwing spears, some firing arrows, some trying to burn him with fire, and some hurling boulders and even mountains at him. Through the force of his concentration, the weapons, rocks, and mountains appeared to him as a rain of fragrant flowers, and the raging fires became like offerings of rainbow lights. With this concentration he removed the final veils of ignorance from his mind and in the next moment became a Buddha, a fully enlightened being. Seeing that

---

5. *Kena Upanishad,* 3–4, as quoted in Paper, *Mystic Experience,* 81.
6. Gyatso, *Introduction to Buddhism,* 8–9.

Siddhartha could not be frightened into abandoning his meditation, Devaputra Mara tried instead to distract him by manifesting countless beautiful women, but Siddhartha responded by developing even deeper concentration. In this way he triumphed over all the demons of this world, which is why he subsequently became known as a "Conqueror Buddha." Siddhartha then continued with his meditation until dawn, when he attained the varja-like concentration.

7. The Annunciation to Mary[7]

In the sixth month the angel Gabriel was sent by God to a town in Galilee called Nazareth, to a virgin engaged to a man whose name was Joseph, of the house of David. The virgin's name was Mary. And he came to her and said, "Greetings, favored one! The Lord is with you." But she was much perplexed by his words and pondered what sort of greeting this might be. The angel said to her, "Do not be afraid, Mary, for you have found favor with God. And now, you will conceive in your womb and bear a son, and you will name him Jesus. He will be great, and will be called the Son of the Most High, and the Lord God will give to him the throne of his ancestor David. He will reign over the house of Jacob forever, and of his kingdom there will be no end." Mary said to the angel, "How can this be, since I am a virgin?" The angel said to her, "The Holy Spirit will come upon you, and the power of the Most High will overshadow you; therefore the child to be born will be holy; he will be called Son of God. And now, your relative Elizabeth in her old age has also conceived a son; and this is the sixth month for her who was said to be barren. For nothing will be impossible with God." Then Mary said, "Here am I, the servant of the Lord; let it be with me according to your word." Then the angel departed from her.

---

7. Luke 1:26–38 NRSV.

Examples of Mystical Experiences

8. The Transfiguration[8]

Six days later, Jesus took with him Peter and James and his brother John and led them up a high mountain, by themselves. And he was transfigured before them, and his face shone like the sun, and his clothes became dazzling white. Suddenly there appeared to them Moses and Elijah, talking with him. Then Peter said to Jesus, "Lord, it is good for us to be here; if you wish, I will make three dwellings here, one for you, one for Moses, and one for Elijah." While he was still speaking, suddenly a bright cloud overshadowed them, and from the cloud a voice said, "This is my Son, the Beloved; with him I am well pleased; listen to him!" When the disciples heard this, they fell to the ground and were overcome by fear. But Jesus came and touched them, saying, "Get up and do not be afraid." And when they looked up, they saw no one except Jesus himself alone.

9. Paul's Conversion on the Road to Damascus[9]

Meanwhile Saul, still breathing threats and murder against the disciples of the Lord, went to the high priest and asked him for letters to the synagogues at Damascus, so that if he found any who belonged to the Way, men or women, he might bring them bound to Jerusalem. Now as he was going along and approaching Damascus, suddenly a light from heaven flashed around him. He fell to the ground and heard a voice saying to him, "Saul, Saul, why do you persecute me?" He asked, "Who are you, Lord?" The reply came, "I am Jesus, whom you are persecuting. But get up and enter the city, and you will be told what you are to do." The men who were traveling with him stood speechless because they heard the voice but saw no one. Saul got up from the ground, and though his eyes were open, he could see nothing; so they led him by the hand and brought him into Damascus. For three days he was without sight, and neither ate nor drank.

8. Matt 17:1–8 NRSV.
9. Acts 9:1–19 NRSV.

Now there was a disciple in Damascus named Ananias. The Lord said to him in a vision, "Ananias." He answered, "Here I am, Lord." The Lord said to him, "Get up and go to the street called Straight, and at the house of Judas look for a man of Tarsus named Saul. At this moment he is praying, and he has seen in a vision a man named Ananias come in and lay his hands on him so that he might regain his sight." But Ananias answered, "Lord, I have heard from many about this man, how much evil he has done to your saints in Jerusalem; and here he has authority from the chief priests to bind all who invoke your name." But the Lord said to him, "Go, for he is an instrument whom I have chosen to bring my name before Gentiles and kings and before the people of Israel; I myself will show him how much he must suffer for the sake of my name." So Ananias went and entered the house. He laid his hands on Saul and said, "Brother Saul, the Lord Jesus, who appeared to you on your way here, has sent me so that you may regain your sight and be filled with the Holy Spirit." And immediately something like scales fell from his eyes, and his sight was restored. Then he got up and was baptized, and after taking some food, he regained his strength.

10. Peter's Dream and Cornelius's Vision[10]

In Caesarea there was a man named Cornelius, a centurion of the Italian Cohort, as it was called. He was a devout man who feared God with all his household; he gave alms generously to the people and prayed constantly to God. One afternoon at about three o'clock he had a vision in which he clearly saw an angel of God coming in and saying to him, "Cornelius." He stared at him in terror and said, "What is it, Lord?" He answered, "Your prayers and your alms have ascended as a memorial before God. Now send men to Joppa for a certain Simon who is called Peter; he is lodging with Simon, a tanner, whose house is by the seaside." When the angel who spoke to him had left, he called two of his slaves and a devout soldier

---

10. Acts 10:1–16 NRSV.

from the ranks of those who served him, and after telling them everything, he sent them to Joppa.

11. St. Perpetua: Dream before Martyrdom[11]

During this calm interlude, Perpetua received a vision that prepared her to face her death courageously. In her mind's eye, she saw a bronze ladder extending to heaven. It was narrow and its sides were lined with hooks, knives, and other sharp tools. So to make the climb, a person had to proceed with great care. A huge serpent lurked at the base of the ladder to terrify people and prevent them from ascending. In the vision, Saturus, the instructor, climbed the ladder of martyrdom before Perpetua. When he reached the top, he turned to encourage her and to warn her about the serpent. "In the name of Jesus Christ," she heard herself declare, "he will not hurt me." Perpetua made the serpent's head her first step, and it cowered under her foot. Then she climbed the ladder unharmed. Thousands clad in white welcomed her into a beautiful garden. A tall man in shepherd's garb said, "Welcome, child," and gave her deliciously sweet milk curds to eat. When the vision ended, Perpetua felt strengthened in her resolve to die rather than to betray her faith.

12. The Desert Fathers: Joseph and Lot[12]

Lot went to Joseph and said, "Abba, as far as I can, I keep a moderate rule, with a little fasting, and prayer, and meditation, and quiet: and as far as I can I try to cleanse my heart of evil thoughts. What else should I do?" Then the hermit stood up and spread out his hands to heaven, and his fingers shone like ten flames of fire, and he said, "If you will, you can become all flame."

---

11. Ghezzi, *Mystics and Miracles*, 61–62.
12. Ward, *Desert Fathers*, 131–33.

13. The Desert Fathers: Unnamed Hermit/Rain

A hermit once visited Mount Sinai. When he was going away, a brother met him, and groaned, saying, "Abba, we are afflicted by drought. There has been no rain." He said, "Why don't you pray and ask God for it?" He replied, "We've been praying and asking God constantly, and still there is no rain." The hermit said, "I don't think you are praying earnestly enough. Shall we see whether that is the case? Let us stand and pray together." He stretched out his hands to heaven and prayed; and at once rain fell. The brother was afraid at the sight, and fell down and worshipped him. But the hermit fled from that place.

14. The Desert Fathers: Miraculous Translation[13]

John [not the apostle] who had been exiled by the Emperor Marcion, said, "One day we went into Syria to see Poemen for we wanted to ask him about hardness of heart. But he did not know Greek and we did not have an interpreter. When he saw we were embarrassed, he began to speak in Greek saying, 'The nature of water is soft, the nature of stone is hard; but if a bottle is hung above a stone letting water drip down, it wears away the stone. It is like that with the word of God; it is soft and our heart is hard, but if a man hears the word of God often, it will break open his heart to the fear of God.'"

15. St. Augustine: Conversion[14]

In my misery I exclaimed: "How long, how long shall I continue to say: 'tomorrow and tomorrow'? Why not now? Why not this very hour put an end to my uncleanness?" This I said, weeping, in the most bitter contrition of my heart. And suddenly I heard a voice from a neighboring house in a singing tune saying and

---

13. Ward, *Desert Fathers*, 191.
14. Augustine, "Confessions," 98.

Examples of Mystical Experiences

often repeating, in the voice of a boy or girl: "Take and read, take and read." Immediately I stopped weeping, and I began to think intently as to whether the singing of words like these was part of any children's game, and I could not remember ever hearing anything like it before. I checked the force of my tears and rose to my feet, interpreting it as nothing other than a divine command to open the book and read the first passage to be found. For I had heard of Anthony [of Egypt] that he happened to enter when the Gospel was being read, and as though the words were spoken directly to himself he accepted the admonition: "Go, sell all that you have and give to the poor, and you shall have treasure in heaven, and come, follow me" (Matt 19:21), and by such an oracle he had been immediately converted to you. So I eagerly returned to that place where Alypius was sitting for there I had left the book of the Apostle [Paul] when I stood up. I snatched the book, opened and read in silence the passage which first met my eye: "Not in rioting and drunkenness, not in chambering and wantonness, not in strife and envying: but put you on the Lord Jesus Christ, and make not provision for the flesh in concupiscence" (Rom. 13:13). I did not want to read further, there was no need to. For as soon as I reached the end of this sentence, it was though my heart was filled with the light of confidence and all the shadows of my doubts were swept away.

16. Mystical Poetry: Taoist[15]

When I looked, my startled eyes saw nothing;
When I listened, no sound met my amazed ear.
Transcending Inaction, I came to Purity,
And entered the neighborhood of the Great Beginning.

---

15. Qu Yuan, fourth century AD, last lines of "Yuan you"; as quoted in Hawkes, *Ch'u-Tz'u*, 97.

Medieval and Early Modern Period (AD 500–1750)

These few examples offer a distinct cross section of the era. Please note the growing personal nature of MEs. Compare these experiences to the more prophetic experiences noted in the Ancient Period that were intended for an entire community.

17. St. Symeon the New Theologian[16]

Suddenly also, falling prostrate on the ground, I saw, and behold! a great light shone intelligibly upon me, attracting my entire mind and soul. I was struck with amazement at the unexpected wonder; I was as in a trance. Nor is this all: I forgot where I was and who I was. I was only content to cry, "*Kyrie eleison*" [Lord, have mercy], so that when I came to my senses, I was surprised to find myself repeating it.... That is not all: suddenly an immense joy, a feeling of the spirit, a sweetness surpassing the savor of any visible thing spread over my soul in an indescribable fashion, granting me a liberty and a forgetfulness of all the thoughts of this life, including the manner of my leaving this present world.... Indeed, all of the feelings of my spirit as well as my soul were attached to the ineffable bliss of this light, of this light alone.

18. Mystical Poetry: Islamic[17]

I saw the sun, moon, stars, and all the lights
...
Everything came toward me—
Nothing remained that did not—
...
Sun and moon were veiled
The stars fell

---

16. As quoted in Krivocheine, *In the Light of Christ*, 217–18.
17. Niffari (d. 965), *Book of Mystical Standings*, as quoted in Sells, "Bewildered Tongue," 111–12.

The lights died out
All save he enveloped in darkness
My eye did not see
My ear did not hear
My perception failed
Everything spoke saying
Allahu Akbar! [God is greatest]

. . .

I fell into the darkness
And beheld myself

19. St. Julian of Norwich: The Hazelnut[18]

And in this he showed me something small, no bigger than a hazelnut, lying in the palm of my hand, as it seemed to me, and it was as round as a ball. I looked at it with the eye of my understanding and thought: What can this be? I was amazed that it could last, for I thought that because of its littleness it would suddenly have fallen into nothing. And I was answered in my understanding: It lasts and always will, because God loves it; and thus everything has being through the love of God. In this little thing I saw three properties. The first is that God made it, the second is that God loves it, the third is that God preserves it. But what did I see in it?

20. St. Joan of Arc: Voices and Visions[19]

In 1424, when Joan was only twelve years old, the great miracle of her life unfolded. One summer day in her father's garden, she heard a mysterious voice, which was accompanied by a bright light. "At first I was very much frightened," she said later. "The voice came toward the hour of noon. I had fasted the preceding day. I heard the voice on my right hand, in the direction of the church. I seldom hear it without seeing a light. The light always

18. Julian of Norwich, *Showings*, 183.
19. Ghezzi, *Mystics and Miracles*, 150–51.

appears on the side from which I hear the voice." She identified the speaker as Michael the Archangel. Subsequently, he spoke to her many times, gradually revealing a preposterous mission. "You have been chosen to restore the kingdom of France," said the voice, "and to protect King Charles." She was to accomplish these things as the head of the army! Imagine the terror and confusion the archangel's messages must have caused young Joan. Michael also told her that St. Catherine and St. Margaret would appear to hear. God was sending these saints, he said, so she must obey their directions. Over the next seven years, Michael, Catherine, and Margaret are said to have visited Joan frequently, sometimes several times a day. Not only could she see and hear her heavenly messengers, but she could also touch and smell them. At her trial she testified that she physically embraced the saints and that they had a pleasant fragrance.

21. St. Teresa of Avila—Pierced by Angels[20]

Our Lord was pleased that I should have at times a vision of this kind: I saw an angel close by me, on my left side, in bodily form. This I am not accustomed to see, unless very rarely. Though I have visions of angels frequently, yet I see them only by an intellectual vision, such as I have spoken of before. It was our Lord's will that in this vision I should see the angel in this wise. He was not large, but small of stature, and most beautiful—his face burning, as if he were one of the highest angels, who seem to be all of fire: they must be those whom we call cherubim. Their names they never tell me; but I see very well that there is in heaven so great a difference between one angel and another, and between these and the others, that I cannot explain it. I saw in his hand a long spear of gold, and at the iron's point there seemed to be a little fire. He appeared to me to be thrusting it at times into my heart and to pierce my very entrails; when he drew it out, he seemed to draw them out also, and to leave me all on fire with a great love of God. The pain

---

20. Teresa of Avila, *Book of Her Life*, 215–16.

was so great, that it made me moan; and yet so surpassing was the sweetness of this excessive pain, that I could not wish to be rid of it. The soul is satisfied now with nothing less than God. The pain is not bodily, but spiritual; though the body has its share in it, even a large one. It is a caressing of love so sweet which now takes place between the soul and God, that I pray God of His goodness to make him experience it who may think that I am lying.

22. Brother Lawrence: Conversion through Nature[21]

The first time I saw brother Lawrence was upon the third of August, 1666. He told me that God had done him a singular favor in this conversion at the age of eighteen. That in the winter, seeing a tree stripped of its leaves, and considering that within a little time the leaves would be renewed, and after that the flowers and fruit appear, he received a high view of the providence and power of God, which has never since been effaced from his soul. That this view had perfectly set him loose from the world, and kindled in him such a love for God that he could not tell whether it had increased during the more than forty years he had lived since.

23. The Conversion of John Wesley[22]

In the evening I went very unwillingly to a society in Aldersgate Street, where one was reading Luther's preface to the Epistle to the Romans. About a quarter before nine, while he was describing the change which God works in the heart through faith in Christ, I felt my heart strangely warmed.

Modern Period (AD 1750-2000)

Stories in this section will likely begin to start sounding more familiar due to the changing language customs that more closely

21. Lawrence, *Practice of the Presence*, 15.
22. Wesley, "Journal," 249-50.

resemble our own. Also, in this section, you'll start to see far more experiences of everyday people. The closer we get to our own era the more likely it is that regular person accounts have been preserved.

24. Mystical Poetry: Christian[23]

Moreover, something is or seems
That touches me with mystic gleams,
Like glimpses of forgotten dreams—

Of something felt, like something here;
Of something done, I know not where;
Such as no language may declare.

25. Few Hallowed Moments[24]

When I walk the fields, I am oppressed now and then with an innate feeling that everything I see has a meaning, if I could but understand it. And this feeling of being surrounded with truths which I cannot grasp amounts to indescribable awe sometimes... Have you not felt that your real soul was imperceptible to your mental vision, expect in a few hallowed moments?

26. I Felt That I Was in Heaven[25]

One brilliant Sunday morning, my wife and boys went to the Unitarian Chapel in Macclesfield. I felt it impossible to accompany them—as though to leave the sunshine on the hills, and go down there to the chapel, would be for the time an act of spiritual suicide.

---

23. Alfred, Lord Tennyson, "The Two Voices," as quoted in James, *Varieties of Religious Experience*, 374.

24. Charles Kingsley, as quoted in James, *Varieties of Religious Experience*, 375–76.

25. John Trevor, as quoted in James, *Varieties of Religious Experience*, 388.

Examples of Mystical Experiences

And I felt such need for new inspiration and expansion in my life. So, very reluctantly and sadly, I left my wife and boys to go down into the town, while I went further up into the hills with my stick and my dog. In the loveliness of the morning, and the beauty of the hills and valleys, I soon lost my sense of sadness and regret. For nearly an hour I walked along the road to the "Cat and Fiddle," and then returned. On the way back, suddenly, without warning, I felt that I was in Heaven—an inward state of peace and joy and assurance indescribably intense, accompanied with a sense of being bathed in a warm glow of light, as though the external condition had brought about the internal effect—a feeling of having passed beyond the body, though the scene around me stood out more clearly and as if nearer to me than before, by reason of the illumination in the midst of which I seemed to be placed. This deep emotion lasted, though with decreasing strength, until I reached home, and for some time after, only gradually passing away.

27. Cosmic Consciousness[26]

I had spent the evening in a great city, with two friends, reading and discussing poetry and philosophy. We parted at midnight. I had a long drive in a hansom to my lodging. My mind, deeply under the influence of the ideas, images, and emotions called up by the reading and talk, was calm and peaceful. I was in a state of quiet, almost passive enjoyment, not actually thinking, but letting ideas, images, and emotions flow of themselves, as it were, through my mind. All at once, without warning of any kind, I found myself wrapped in a flame-colored cloud. For an instant I thought of fire, an immense conflagration somewhere close by in that great city; the next, I knew that the fire was within myself. Directly afterward there came upon me a sense of exultation, of immense joyousness accompanied or immediately followed by an intellectual illumination impossible to describe. Among other things, I did not merely come to believe, but I saw that the universe is not composed of

---

26. Bucke, *Cosmic Consciousness*, 7–8.

dead matter, but is, on the contrary, a living Presence: I became conscious in myself of eternal life, but a consciousness that I possessed eternal life then; I saw that all men are immortal; that the cosmic order is such that without any peradventure [chance] all things work together for the good of each and all; that the foundation principle of the world, of all the worlds, is what we call love, and that the happiness of each and all is in the long run absolutely certain. The vision lasted a few seconds and was gone but the memory of it and the sense of the reality of what it taught has remained during the quarter of a century which has since elapsed. I knew that what the vision showed was true. I had attained to a point of view from which I saw that it must be true. That view, that conviction, I may say that consciousness, has never, even during periods of the deepest depression, been lost.

28. On a Single Point[27]

Sometimes, when I have scrutinized the world very closely I have thought that I could see it enveloped in an atmosphere—still very tenuous but already individualized—of mutual good will and of truths accepted in common and retained as a permanent heritage. I have seen a shadow floating, as though it were the wraith of a universal soul seeking to be born . . . What name can we give to this mysterious Entity, who is in some small way our own handiwork, with whom, eminently, we can enter into communion; who is some part of ourselves, yet who masters us, has need of us in order to exist, and at the same time dominates us with the full force of his Absolute being? I can feel it: he has a name and a face, but he alone can reveal his face and pronounce his name: Jesus! Together with all the beings around me I felt that I was caught up in a higher movement that was stirring together all the elements of the Universe and grouping them in a new order. When it was given to me to see where the dazzling trail of particular beauties and

---

27. Teilhard de Chardin, *Writings in Time of War*, 145–46.

Examples of Mystical Experiences

partial harmonies was leading, I recognized that it was all coming to centre *on a single point*, on a Person: your Person.

29. Escape[28]

One day I had an experience which I did not understand, and will never forget. After lunch I sat at my husband's desk, and saw that he had been doodling on the blotter a tangled mess! I thought it expressed all the difficulties he was experiencing. Can you imagine, the doodling moved, and formed the word "escape"! This was astonishing enough but then "Escape" became an eye, a living luminous eye, which expanded. It was magnetic. It became more and more brilliant as it became larger, until there was nothing but the most unimaginably brilliant living white light, expanded to infinity. I was absorbed into this. You may not be able to believe or understand—I don't understand it myself, because it is a unique experience, which I can't share with anyone I have met, but I know with the same knowing I have described before [she earlier in the letter describes other experiences], that I was absorbed into this wonderful living light, and at this moment I felt the greatest emotion of joy I have ever felt in my life. I lost my physical self and became one with this extraordinary expanding universe of light. I felt very strong and thrilling vibrations that seemed to have no beginning or end but I seemed to stretch out to infinity. Suddenly a shock, which felt like all my physical atoms coming together to form me again, and I was back in this world again. I felt uplifted, rejuvenated, and comforted. How can I ever forget this wonderful experience. [sic] I know it.

---

28. Unnamed person in study, as quoted in Paper, *Mystic Experience*, 13–14.

30. May the Time Come[29]

May the time come when men, having been awakened to a sense of the close bond linking all the movements of this world in the single, all-embracing work of the Incarnation, shall be unable to give themselves to any one of their tasks without illuminating it with the clear vision that their work—however elementary it may be—is received and put to good use by a Centre of the universe. When that comes to pass, there will be little to separate life in the cloister from the life of the world. And only then will the action of the children of heaven (at the same time as the action of the children of the world) have attained the intended plenitude of its humanity.

31. I Seemed to Become This Light[30]

A year ago while going about my normal duties as a housewife, I paused for a moment to see whether my mind was free from all thought about something which has caused me a great deal of unhappiness and pain. My mind was perfectly controlled, and I was just about to give myself a pat on the back and a well-done old girl—when! my vision was completely blacked out and light seemed all about my head—not the daylight—but a light in my mind and around—I could as it were feel the walls of my head crumbling down. I cannot explain the degree of light, there is nothing to compare it with. I seemed to become this light and consciousness of my personal self seemed to be held very faintly and of no consequence—how this light was left behind or how I came out of it I do not know, but there was another light—different—a nothing or void—which I gazed at, or was aware of. There seemed to be nothing in this second light—no body—no sound—empty—and yet I knew it wasn't empty. As quickly as I had merged into light so I once more returned to my duties. When I say I returned of course I know that I didn't go anywhere—all I knew was that the

---

29. Teilhard de Chardin, *Divine Milieu*, 67.
30. Unnamed person in study, as quoted in Paper, *Mystic Experience*, 13.

consciousness was held by some immense power, which made my poor little effort of stout control as nothing.

32. A Perfect Summer Day[31]

In 1972, the most momentous event of my life took place on a perfect summer day at an ideal summer occasion, a weekend folk music/jazz festival on the beautiful park-island that forms the outer boundary of Toronto's harbor. I was assisting a newly befriended couple who crafted leather bags and were selling them from their pushcart, and had met through them that morning a female artist who, with her husband, have remained my closest friends since. It was early afternoon and, having finished a light lunch, I lay down alone on the grass under the shade of an old tree. I was lying on my side and directly in my vision across a sunlit, mown field I perceived an attractive woman. Without moving my head or eyes, I focused on her, enjoying the vision with little or no thought, save a pleasant erotic feeling. At first she slowly filled my vision, as if I were floating toward her or her toward me. Then with increasing speed she came closer and closer, followed by trees, rocks, the field, then the entire universe, whirling in a giant vortex that funneled into me. As everything literally became one with me, I perceived a bright light inside rather than outside of me. This light can best be described as white, but it was all colors simultaneously, and it was bright beyond the brightest light imaginable. I, the universe, began to fly faster and faster toward this light. At the moment, I comprehended that I had to make an instantaneous decision: I could enter the light into which I would merge and be gone or stop and end the experience. Somehow, I recognized what was happening; I sped into the light and dissolved in an immense flood tide of joy.

---

31. Unnamed person in study, as quoted in Paper, *Mystic Experience*, 1.

Thinking Spiritually in Small Groups

33. Staying in the Church Overnight[32]

I had decided that I would stay in the church overnight, just to be doing it [staying in the church overnight]. I went to one of the social rooms where there was a couch and settled myself, hearing the preacher leave for home and knowing the church was now empty. After a bit as I sat, it was just beginning to lose some of the light, but the room was still very light, I began to observe without seeing anything and hear without actually hearing anything, a circular movement start in the upper right hand corner of the room. This movement grew louder and with it a roar (not audible). There was [a] tremendous feeling of an impersonal power entering the room, a power that belonged here and was oblivious to me. By the time the movement had reached halfway across the room and the roar had gathered a power to go with it, I was so frightened I realized that this was God coming, and nothing could stand in His way, and that I was utterly unprepared to meet Him and utterly unworthy and if I stayed I would likely lose my mind, and I got up and ran out of the church.

34. Voice in the Car[33]

From that day forward my desire to get drunk was completely gone! Having attempted to quit drinking on several occasions before and experiencing how difficult it was, I came to realize that God had done something supernatural to be bring me through this. He had done a real miracle in my life... Driving from Savage to Laurel, Maryland, on February fifteenth, I heard a voice in my car which seemed to come from every direction. I looked into the back seat to see if someone was hiding in the back seat. No one was there. I won't go into all the details of the next few moments, but in summary, this voice told me that Jesus Christ was going to come into my life. I did not understand the meaning of what was going

---

32. Paper, *Mystic Experience*, 18–19.

33. Unnamed person in study, as quoted in Bridgers, *Contemporary Varieties of Religious Experience*, 145–46.

Examples of Mystical Experiences

on so I argued with Whoever [sic] was speaking to me that such a thing couldn't happen. In attempting to argue with this Voice (for I didn't see a person with it) I noticed that Whoever I was speaking with had the answers to my thoughts before I could actually bring them to my conscience [sic]. It was a terrifying experience. I felt completely undone. I was afraid to even think. I finally told this Voice that He could do whatever He wanted, but to just go away, leave me alone. For the next three days after this incident I walked this earth in what seemed to be perfect love. I think it was absolutely impossible for me during that time to hate anyone, not even the most evil person I could think of. I felt like a small child holding on to the back of Jesus, looking at the world through His eyes, hearing with His ears, and loving with His heart. For three days this earth was paradise. Everything was beautiful.

35. Music and LIGHT[34]

I was at a concert with a friend, given by the Hallé orchestra. They were playing the Chorale Symphony (Beethoven) and as I did not know the music well, I retreated into my own thoughts—which were pretty depressing. I prayed to be taken out of the "black pit of my own mind and selfishness" and suddenly, in answer, there was a rush of LIGHT, which surrounded me, lifted me into LIGHT and at the same time seemed to melt my physical being so that LIGHT welled up also from within me, or rather, burst out of me, to meet the LIGHT that was without. With this LIGHT came BLISS, happiness a million times stronger than anything I had ever experienced on earth: and on earth I had been, at times, completely happy. At the same time, I felt a cool breeze playing on me, and within me a whirling sensation and a feeling that I was somehow above myself—my body—but not completely, only a foot or so.

---

34. Unnamed person in study, as quoted in Paper, *Mystic Experience*, 21.

36. I Was Aware[35]

It was in the spring this year [1988] I was resting on our settee with my legs up. I can't recall if I was praying, but I think not, certainly I was aware. The window is across the room and gently this glorious light built up in front of the window growing ever brighter and larger until I was enveloped within it and felt myself raised up into it. At the same time there was what I can only describe as a "noiseless noise"—very beautiful. I knew it was heavenly and I was filled with delight and awe, no fear. I tried to see the face of Jesus, because I felt it was of him, but could not. I was lowered down and the light withdrew as it had come.

37. Dances at the Pueblos[36]

I was at the dances at one of the pueblos. The drums pounded into my chest, connected me with the stamp of the dancers' feet. The drums pounded on and on, lulling me into their rhythm. I can't explain it. I can't find the words to use. But for a moment, an unforgettable instant that cold, clear Christmas day, I became the drums. Something happened. One second I was myself, quietly, respectfully watching the dances, as I did every Christmas day. Then the pulse of the drum became my heartbeat. The pulse of the drums became the rhythm of life, the beat of all time, and the lines separating me from the adobe walls, from the earth, the sky and the dancers, disappeared. For a moment there was only the drums, only the pulse of all that is. How long did it last? A moment? A minute? Perhaps a couple of minutes. It was a place that had no time, but in that instant, whatever its length, I understood the drums, understood their language, their necessity, the connection between observer and observed, between objective and subjective. A moment later I found myself again, in the same place, in the same position, irrevocably changed. My cheek still leaned against

---

35. Unnamed person in study, as quoted in Paper, *Mystic Experience*, 21.

36. Unnamed person in study, as quoted in Bridgers, *Contemporary Varieties of Religious Experience*, 164.

the cool rough surface of the adobe wall, my sheepskin coat still wrapped warmly around me. Looking up, my eyes met a wedge of geese, flying low over the pueblo, giving even the sanction of the sky to the pueblo below.

38. A Cosmic Thunderbolt[37]

The beginning of the experience was very sudden and dramatic, I was hit by a cosmic thunderbolt of immense power that instantly shattered and dissolved my everyday reality. I completely lost contact with the surrounding world; it disappeared as if by magic . . . At that time, my only reality was a mass of swirling energy of immense proportions that seemed to contain all of Existence in an entirely abstract form. It had the brightness of myriads of suns, yet it was not on the same continuum with any light I knew from everyday life . . . I had no categories for what I was witnessing. I could not maintain a sense of separate existence in the face of such a force. My ordinary identity was shattered and dissolved; I became one with the Source. Time lost any meaning whatsoever.

39. Before and After[38]

I was still crying . . . when I felt two strong hands reach under my arms and pull me gently upward. I had the impression that I was being lifted out of my body, which was still kneeling on the floor. I felt connected to it, in a distant way, but not inside it. It was only, after all, a woman of earth, wrapped around a child of earth. I, the part of me that constitutes my identity, was lifted away from it, into an embrace so sweet that for years it never for a single second left my mind. Still today, when I hear a song on the radio about finding the ultimate love, the perfect love, the love one cannot live without, I think about the being who picked me up and held me like a baby,

---

37. Grof, *Cosmic Game*, 28.
38. Unnamed person in study, as quoted in Bridgers, *Contemporary Varieties of Religious Experience*, 165.

on that chilly spring night near Harvard Square. I don't know how long it lasted; maybe thirty seconds, maybe ten minutes. Not more than that. Whatever it was, my entire existence still hinges on that brief encounter. It is the center point for me, the single event that divides my life into Before and After.

Current (AD 2000-present)

Almost all of these accounts come from persons who have been in one or more of my mystical reflection groups, used with permission. As a result, the tone of these accounts may move more in the direction of a journal or diary entry.

40. Nature Illuminated[39]

I can recount one such story from a few years back. I was walking in a park near my home, as I often do, savoring the colors and textures of the leaves, responding to the unique "personalities" of different kinds of trees that overarched the pathway, noticing the birds and butterflies as my fellow creatures. This is not at all unusual for me; this how I "live and move and have my being" in God—to walk as a creature among creatures in God's wonderful creation, with my heart open to the Creator, practicing God's presence with me. But on this occasion, for a period of about twenty minutes, I felt that every tree, every blade of grass, and every pool of water became especially eloquent to God's grandeur. Somehow they seemed to become transparent—or perhaps translucent is the better word—because each thing in its particularity was still utterly visible and unspeakably important: the movement of the grass in waves swayed by the wind, the way the goldfinches perch just so on a purple thistle plant. These specific, concrete things became translucent in the sense that a powerful, indescribable, invisible light seemed to shine through. The beauty of the creation around

---

39. McLaren, *Generous Orthodoxy*, 177-78.

me, which I am always careful to notice, seemed on this day to explode, seemed to detonate, seemed to radiate with glory.

41. Centering Prayer—Crackling Ball of Energy (Compilation of Multiple MEs)[40]

I felt impressed yesterday to center using the word *return*. In using this word, I couldn't help picturing sitting before a huge ball of crackling white energy, then I was inside this ball, and then I looked up and a huge ray of energy shot up toward heaven. At this point, I was filled with a sense of love, peace, wonder, and astounding potential (though not necessarily my own potential). Maybe, I'm just letting my imagination run away with me, but it was very ... enlightening, all the same.

...

When I center, a persistent vision appears, well, with a few variations. I sense a ball of crackling white (or dark) energy at the core of my being (i.e., center of my upper abdomen) that I intuit as the goodness of the image of God or, to be more traditional, the ground of my soul. I then imagine my true self (though often in shadow) as sitting or standing before it, or sometimes entering within, or even traveling through it infinitely.

...

A fleeting image—from that great ball of crackling energies, hope flows into me as blinding white rays of light. This light illuminates me and shines through me. Wisdom also is present in this flow of hope, giving substance and tangibility to the light.

...

For the past few days, I've been experimenting with the use of an image in centering prayer along with the focus of my sacred word *listen*. I think it is helping me to center—

For instance, I saw this morning in my mind's eye that great, big crackle ball of energy, and I was sitting quietly in front of it (for some reason, I can never picture images in centering prayer from

---

40. Experience communicated by mystical reflection participant.

a first-person perspective—I always see myself in front of it too). For a long time, I meditated on the undulating lights and pulses of energy, then I touched the ball and that energy and light began to pulse through me as well. At that moment, I became aware of my own breathing and of God's Spirit pulsing and energizing in the same ways as these images.

. . .

As I prayed today, I saw something in my mind's eye. I was sitting before the ball of crackling energy which I so often see/imagine in my prayers. All of a sudden the ball radiated bright pink energy, illuminating everything. Somehow, I knew this color of energy signified love. I approached the energy ball and was illuminated by it. The funny thing is that I was still a silhouette—all shape and shadow, no detail, no content. With outline still transforming, hazy, and indistinct, I approached the ball of energy. Suddenly, it flowed into me—all of it—and the radiance burned within me and glimmered out through me. Then, the ball was back where it was—still the same size, shape, and radiance that it had when it first blazed pink. It was almost as if I were seeing that love poured out does not exhaust itself—it only burns brighter and goes further.

42. Centering Prayer—Oneness (Compilation of Multiple MEs)[41]

There are times when I sense, whether in reality or only in the eye of my imagination, that the distinct separateness of all things is breached, and I am one with all things, radiating out from where I physically sit. This feeling does not destroy the uniqueness of anything, even myself; rather, I'm touched profoundly that we are all connected . . . mystically connected.

. . .

Early on in this session of centering prayer, a helpful image rolled through my head. As I breathed in, I could see in my mind's eye a bright blue ball of energy at the core of my being. As I breathed

---

41. Experience communicated by mystical reflection participant.

Examples of Mystical Experiences

out, the ball stretched out into thousands of tiny tendrils extending to everyone and everything around me. This energy is hope.

...

A few days ago, as I centered with the word *welcome*, I had the strange sense of the word echoing in my mind with the sound of many voices. Simultaneously, I had a brief brush with a sense of connection to the surrounding environment—all of this in the space of a few moments.

43. Centering Prayer—Physical Effects[42]

This tidbit may not seem to be worth mentioning, but I thought that it might be interesting or important for me or someone else to remember somewhere down the road—Occasionally, while centering, I have a sense for a few moments of dizziness then unbelievable lightness, as if I'm floating. Soon thereafter, when I think of my sacred word, everything floods back to normal. This sensation doesn't seem to have an easily discernible purpose although I usually feel quite refreshed afterward.

44. *Lectio Divina*

Yesterday, part of my *lectio [Divina]* passage was a portion of Psalm 72 which reads—"Be rainfall on cut grass, earth-refreshing rain showers. Let righteousness burst into blossom and peace abound until the moon fades to nothing" [*The Message* version]. Yesterday afternoon and all evening a gentle, soaking rain fell—little things.[43]

45. Centering Prayer—Not Too Seriously[44]

On multiple occasions as I attempted to center, my wife texted me pictures of our infant son sitting in a pot—happy as can be with a

---

42. Experience communicated by mystical reflection participant.
43. Experience communicated by mystical reflection participant.
44. Experience communicated by mystical reflection participant.

huge smile on his face. As I began to pray again after these "interruptions," God brushed my mind with this thought: "Maybe, the holiest thing for you today is to see your son sitting in a pot." Don't take yourself too seriously.

46. Centering Prayer—Intellectual Vision (Father and Son)[45]

Fleeting image arising while praying with the word *presence*—
A boy and father at a bathroom mirror—the boy is five or six and "shaving" for the first time. He is full of pride and delight at being so grown-up with such joy at getting to shave "with Daddy." The father is full of hope and pride in his son, and he also knows that he has taken the blade out of the razor. The father hopes because he sees his son in the process of becoming and knowing he has so many adventures ahead of him. The son has so much joy and pride in that moment, in that experience, with Daddy—That is presence.

47. Centering Prayer—Synchronicity/Coincidence[46]

Some odd thoughts during prayer today . . . I saw myself teaching English to younger students (high school? younger?) and distinctly had the impression "Teach them like your own children."

[Interestingly, the participant who recorded this account did start a job teaching English to junior high students about five years later.]

48. Centering Prayer—God Is the Wind[47]

God is the wind, and we cannot see him, but on a windy day—with all that blowing dust—it is stimulating to think that we see God by how he moves the dust of the earth, humanity, us . . . Watch . . .

   45. Experience communicated by mystical reflection participant.
   46. Experience communicated by mystical reflection participant.
   47. Experience communicated by mystical reflection participant.

49. Labyrinth/Centering Prayer[48]

As I walked the labyrinth, I found myself centering with the word *possibility*, and I noted that the winding path led to one center at which one could look to every corner of the world. When I had walked back to the beginning of the labyrinth (and symbolically to the re-entry point of the world), this prayer formed within me: "O God, Beautiful and Infinite, Mighty All-Father and Ever-Wise, may endless possibility give birth to beautiful realities. To the glory of the Father and the Son and the Spirit. As it was in the beginning, is now, and ever shall be. World without end. May it be."

50. Ladybug—Synchronicity Experience[49]

One night at community Eucharist I noticed a ladybug on the floor in the center aisle of the church. It made me sad because I was sure that when church was over, people were going to leave by that center aisle and the ladybug would be crushed, not maliciously, just by accident. I recognized in myself a fear of that same kind of random misfortune happening to me. I feel it strongly in this season of life where our lives and my husband's livelihood are in the hands of others, who don't know or care about us on a personal level. I shared these thoughts with my husband after church. The next day, he sent me this message: "During MP [Morning Prayer] today I saw one of those Japanese beetles in the middle of the aisle and was thinking about what you were saying when I heard this read from Isaiah: 'Do not fear, you worm Jacob, you insect Israel! I will help you, says the Lord; your redeemer is the Holy One of Israel.'" It felt like a specific response to the fear and sadness I had felt and expressed the day before in church.

---

48. Experience communicated by mystical reflection participant.
49. Experience communicated by mystical reflection participant.

51. Never Lonely Again[50]

The mystical experience I want to share with you here began on Highway 51 in Charlotte, NC, in a Plymouth Acclaim, probably 10:00 o'clock [sic] at night. I was seventeen. I had just returned from a youth conference, a spiritual retreat that I had been to several times before. We'd been working hard in the weeks leading up [to] it, making the out-of-town trip a few times to plan and prepare. This weekend we'd worked, played, sang, prayed, and stayed up too late ministering to one another as best we knew how. I don't remember the two-hour drive from the conference back to Charlotte. I'm sure we stopped to eat at our favorite spot and swapped stories from the weekend. Back in Charlotte, at the church we all met at a few days earlier, we told each other one last time how much we love one another, that we'll get together soon, and that we can't wait to do it again. I climbed in my car and pulled out onto the road, the endless streetlights illuminating the broad, empty road. A wave of feeling came over me, and I began crying, sobbing actually. The streetlight refracted and blurred so that I could hardly see the road. (This was my first adult cry, not from skinning a knee or getting spanked.) I was utterly alone, but I was crying because I wasn't lonely. The warmth, love, and confidence from the community I'd just left was still with me, and I knew I'd never be lonely again. When I pulled into my driveway, my mom was waiting in the carport. She saw my tears and asked me if I was OK. I told her I was, I really was. She believed me and let me be. I went to my room, buried my face in my pillow, and cried for an hour, repeating "God, I love you. I love you so much."

52. Ash Wednesday Mystical Experience[51]

I had a mystical experience in the Ash Wednesday service last night. As the sermon began, my attention began to wander first to one stained glass window then another and another. Eventually,

---

50. Experience communicated by mystical reflection participant.
51. Experience communicated by mystical reflection participant.

Examples of Mystical Experiences

my gaze rested on a window that had Lady Wisdom (Sophia) as the central figure. As I looked, she seemed to grow brighter and "shimmer" like heat waves coming off the road on a hot summer day. Also, everything else became dimmer, fuzzier—while she was in crystal clear focus. The preacher continued to drone on, but he sounded further away somehow. At that point, I heard in my mind (not audibly) a voice saying, "She will lead you into all truth." As the moment ended, I realized that I was having a mystical experience as I was having it. My feelings in that moment and immediately following were subtle elation, contentment, and gentle peace. The entire experience couldn't have lasted more than a minute or two. Then, it was back to the real world and the third (if I remember correctly) of three points in the preacher's sermon. The experience began at some moment after the preacher began to dig into his first point.

53. Spark[52]

I had a "little" mystical experience at church this morning. Today was the bishop's annual visit. There was a baptism, two reaffirmations, and a renewal. The bishop also preached a fantastic sermon. However, none of that resonated much with me. My attention was elsewhere (or perhaps else*when*). Soon after arriving at church and sitting down in the pew, my attention was drawn to the sanctuary candle at the front corner. Now, I'm sure it has been there and been burning every time I had been at church. That's part of its purpose after all. Still, it had never caught my eye before today. This morning I couldn't seem to take my eyes off of it. I was mesmerized by the dance and flicker of that tiny flame. I even saw all of the area surrounding the candle and its holder "shimmer" as well. Within, I sensed the word *spark* in connection with that candle, but its meaning is deeper than that surface sense alone. It was only a few minutes although I felt my eyes drawn back to that flickering spark throughout the service.

---

52. Experience communicated by mystical reflection participant.

54. Power Nap[53]

I had just come home from work, and I decided to take a quick power nap on my sofa before anyone came home from work or school. I was awoken with the very clear words, "What does this mean?" I immediately opened my eyes. The only thing in my line of vision was the solitary crucifix that hung on a slender piece of wall.

55. Ask Your Question[54]

This dream began with me hiking through a rain forest somewhere in Asia with my twelve brothers. I do not have twelve brothers in real life, but I did have twelve brothers in this dream. As we were hiking through the rain forest, we came upon a hut. It was almost like a temple where people were worshipping. There was an androgynous person sitting on top of a tall chair, kind of like the type of chair that a lifeguard sits on. I related to this person as a woman more than a man, but the person had long hair, eye liner, feminine facial features, and a man's muscular, bare chest. People were worshipping this person. I stayed away. I was very skeptical even though I was just a little curious. While I was in the back of the crowd watching everything that was happening, the androgynous person caught my eye, and I caught their eye. The person gave me a very knowing look. Someone came out from the building and told everyone that it was time to go, and the androgynous person climbed down and went inside the building. I recollected my brothers, and we began to leave. We were no longer in a rain forest, but we were now in a city. As we were walking away, a person was sneaking out of the side door of the building. It was the androgynous person, though the person seemed more like a woman at this point in the dream. The person looked at me and said, "I like your pants." Again, I was hesitant to interact, but I said "thank you." The person said, "Why don't you ask your question?" I was bothered

---

53. Experience communicated by mystical reflection participant.
54. Experience communicated by mystical reflection participant.

by this question because the person was able to sense my curiosity. I said, "I don't know what you are talking about." The person said again, "Ask your question." Again, I insisted that I did not have a question. One final time, the person said, "Ask your question." And, again, I said that I did not have a question. The person looked at me with curious eyes, and said "Let's go inside and bring your twelve brothers." We went inside the building and talked on and on and on for what seemed like hours. I don't know what we talked about, but we were sitting in a little breakfast-nook-type-place with windows all around, and we were drinking tea. As we talked, the sun began to rise, and I woke up.

56. You Walk among Them[55]

I was almost nine months pregnant with our first child at the time of my first auditory mystical experience. My husband and I decided to practice centering prayer together one evening. As I was praying, I was pretty tired, and I fell asleep toward the end of the prayer session. I was awakened, not by the sound of the gong or by my husband, but by these words ringing in my ears, "You walk among them."

---

55. Experience communicated by mystical reflection participant.

Bibliography

Alston, William P. "Mysticism and the Perpetual Awareness of God." In *The Blackwell Guide to the Philosophy of Religion*, edited by William E. Mann, 198–219. Malden, MA: Blackwell, 2005.

Augustine, St. "The Confessions (Books 7–10)." In *Augustine of Hippo: Selected Writings*, translated by Mary T. Clark, 55–162. Classics of Western Spirituality. New York: Paulist, 1984.

Bridgers, Lynn. *Contemporary Varieties of Religious Experience: James's Classic Study in Light of Resilience, Temperament, and Trauma*. Lanham, MD: Rowman & Littlefield, 2005.

Bucke, Richard M. *Cosmic Consciousness: A Study in the Evolution of the Human Mind*. Philadelphia: Innes & Sons, 1901.

The Cloud of Unknowing. Edited by James Walsh. Classics of Western Spirituality. Ramsey, NJ: Paulist, 1981.

Corbin, Juliet, and Anselm Strauss. *Basics of Qualitative Research: Techniques and Procedures for Developing Grounded Theory*. 3rd ed. Thousand Oaks, CA: Sage, 2008.

De Mello, Anthony. *The Song of the Bird*. New York: Doubleday, 1984.

Dougherty, Mary. *Group Spiritual Direction: Community for Discernment*. New York: Paulist, 1995.

Forem, Jack. *Transcendental Meditation: The Essential Teachings of Maharishi Mahesh Yogi*. Rev. ed. Carlsbad, CA: Hay House, 2012.

Fryling, Alice. *Seeking God Together: An Introduction to Group Spiritual Direction*. Downers Grove, IL: InterVarsity, 2009.

Ghezzi, Bert. *Mystics and Miracles: True Stories of Lives Touched by God*. Chicago: Loyola, 2004.

Grof, Stanislav. *The Cosmic Game: Explorations of the Frontiers of Human Consciousness*. Albany, NY: SUNY Press, 1998.

Guenther, Margaret. *Holy Listening: The Art of Spiritual Direction*. Lanham, MD: Rowman & Littlefield, 1992.

Gyatso, Geshe Kelsang. *Introduction to Buddhism: An Explanation of the Buddhist Way of Life*. Glen Spey, NY: Tharpa, 2016.

Bibliography

Hair, Gerald. "Three Basic Questions for the Guide." In *Sharing Sacred Stories: Current Approaches to Spiritual Direction and Guidance*, edited by Robert Frager, 70–71. New York: Crossroad, 2007.

Hawkes, David. *Ch'u-Tz'u: The Songs of the South*. London: Oxford University Press, 1959.

Heimlich, Russell. "Mystical Experiences." *Pew Research Center*, December 29, 2009. https://www.pewresearch.org/fact-tank/2009/12/29/mystical-experiences/.

Hopcke, Robert H. "Spiritual Direction and Mystical Experience." In *Sharing Sacred Stories: Current Approaches to Spiritual Direction and Guidance*, edited by Robert Frager, 86–88. New York: Crossroad, 2007.

Howe, Gregory Michael, custodian. *The Book of Common Prayer and Administration of the Sacraments and Other Rites and Ceremonies of the Church: Together with the Psalter or Psalms of David; According to the Use of the Episcopal Church*. New York: Church, 1979, 2007.

Huxley, Aldous. *The Perennial Philosophy*. New York: Harper, 2009.

James, William. *Varieties of Religious Experience: A Study in Human Nature*. New York: Random House, 1902.

John of the Cross, St. *Selected Writings*. Translated by Kieran Kavanaugh. Classics of Western Spirituality. New York: Paulist, 1987.

Julian of Norwich. *Showings*. Translated by Edmund Colledge and James Walsh. Classics of Western Spirituality. New York: Paulist, 1978.

Kabat-Zinn, Jon. *Full Catastrophe Living: Using the Wisdom of the Body and Mind to Face Stress, Pain, and Illness*. New York: Bantam, 2013.

Kamdar, Rushabh. "Infantile Amnesia." *International Journal of Science and Research* 5.11 (November 2016) 28–30.

Keating, Thomas. *Open Mind, Open Heart: The Contemplative Dimension of the Gospel*. New York: Continuum, 1997.

Krivocheine, Basil. *In the Light of Christ: Saint Symeon the New Theologian (949–1022), Life, Spirituality, Doctrine*. Translated by Anthony P. Gythiel. Crestwood, NY: St. Vladimir's Seminary Press, 1986.

Law, Eric H. F. *The Bush Was Blazing but Not Consumed*. St Louis: Chalice, 1996.

Lawrence, Brother. *The Practice of the Presence of God with Spiritual Maxims*. Grand Rapids: Spire, 1967.

Mavrodes, George. "Real v. Deceptive Mystical Experiences." In *Mysticism and Philosophical Analysis*, edited by Steven T. Katz, 235–58. New York: Oxford University Press, 1978.

McLaren, Brian. *A Generous Orthodoxy*. Grand Rapids: Zondervan, 2004.

Paper, Jordan. *The Mystic Experience: A Descriptive and Comparative Analysis*. Albany: SUNY Press, 2004.

Pennington, M. Basil. *Centering Prayer: Renewing an Ancient Christian Prayer Form*. New York: Image, 2001.

Sells, Michael A. "Bewildered Tongue: The Semantics of Mystical Union in Islam." In *Mystical Union and Monotheistic Faith: An Ecumenical*

Bibliography

Dialogue, edited by Moshe Idel and Bernard McGinn, 111–12. New York: MacMillan, 1989.

Teilhard de Chardin, Pierre. *The Divine Milieu*. Edited by Bernard Wall. New York: Harper & Row, 1968.

———. *Writings in Time of War*. Translated by René Hague. New York: Harper & Row, 1968.

Teresa of Avila, St. *The Book of Her Life*. Edited by Benedict Zimmerman. Translated by Davis Lewis. New York: Benziger, 1911.

Uehara, Izumi. "Developmental Changes in Memory-Related Linguistic Skills and Their Relationship to Episodic Recall in Children." *PLoS One* 10.9 (September 2015) 1–24.

Ward, Benedicta. *The Desert Fathers: Sayings of the Early Christian Monks*. New York: Penguin, 2003.

Wesley, John. "Journal: May 24, 1738." In *Collected Works* 18, edited by W. Reginald Ward and Richard P. Heitzenrater, 249–50. Nashville: Abingdon, 1988.

Wigner, Dann. *Just Begin: A Sourcebook of Spiritual Practices*. New York: Church, 2018.

———. *A Sociology of Mystic Practices: Use and Adaptation in the Emergent Church*. Eugene, OR: Pickwick, 2018.

Index

acceptance, 45, 55
active listening 42, 55–56, 59–61
analogy 10, 12–15, 17, 20, 24, 56
angel(s) 76–78, 80, 82, 88
Augustine, Saint, 84

Bible, 7, 23, 70
Book of Common Prayer, The, 34, 47, 64
Buddha, 79–80

centering prayer, vii, 1, 6, 21–23, 25–32, 38–40, 42–45, 66–67, 70–72, 74–75, 101–5, 109
Chardin, Teilhard de, 92, 94
check-in, 33–35, 49, 56, 69
childcare, 32, 39, 63–64, 68
choiceless awareness, 44
cloud of unknowing, 13–14
coincidence(s), 5, 48, 68, 76, 104
compassionate communication, 59–61
confidentiality, 55, 61–62
consciousness, 19, 44, 68, 91–92, 94–95
consensus, 39, 52, 60, 68, 71
contemplation, 19, 24–25
continuum, 6, 18–19, 99
customization, 36–38, 49, 51, 54, 68, 71

dark night of the soul, 53

Desert Fathers, the, 83–84
dream(s), x, 15, 19, 65–68, 75–76, 78, 82–83, 90, 108

episodic memory, 11
evaluation(s), 51–52, 58–59, 62–63, 72
expectation(s), 35, 50–53, 55, 72

fleeting, 10, 14–15, 17, 19–20, 101, 104
hazelnut, 87
heaven, 76, 81, 83–85, 88, 90–91, 94, 98, 101
Hindu, 79
Holy Spirit, 2, 55, 80, 82

incarnation, 94
induce/inducing, 44, 53
ineffability, 10, 12–15, 17, 20
interpreting/interpretation, 4–5, 16–17, 41–42, 45–46, 52, 55–57, 66, 68, 71, 84–85
interruptive/interruption, 17, 39, 60, 104
intimate vulnerability, 62
Islamic, 86

Jacob (biblical figure), 76–78, 80, 105
James, William, 8–10, 13–14, 16–20, 90

115

Index

Jesus (biblical figure), 34, 47, 64, 70, 80–83, 85, 92, 96–98
Joan of Arc, Saint, 87–88
Joseph (biblical figure), 78, 80, 83
Julian of Norwich, Saint, 87
Just Begin, ix, 5, 10, 16, 25, 28, 44

Keating, Thomas, 25–26, 38

labyrinth, 5, 75, 105
ladybug, 105
language acquisition, 11
Lawrence, Brother, 89
logistical, 50–51, 55, 63, 72

Mary (biblical figure), 80
messy, 43
monasticism, 25
Moses (biblical figure), 52, 78, 81
mystical practice(s), 2, 5–6, 10, 16–17, 20–23, 25, 44, 74

noetic quality, 10, 13–15, 17, 20
nondirective, 54
note card(s), 41, 44
oneness, 75, 102

passivity, 10, 15–17, 20
Paul (biblical figure), 81, 85
Pennington, M. Basil, 25–26, 38
Perpetua, Saint, 83
perspective, 13–15, 17, 20, 45–47, 53, 57, 60, 66, 68, 71, 102
Peter (biblical figure), 81–82
pilot groups, 6–7
practical, 8, 10, 22, 25–26, 35, 50–51, 60, 63, 71
pragmatic, 7
Prayer for Guidance, vii, 31, 34–35, 47, 64, 67, 69, 71

Pseudo-Dionysius, 13

rainbow, 20, 79

safe space, 6, 32–33, 43, 55–56, 59, 62, 72, 74
silent/silence, 3, 25–26, 32, 38–39, 43, 51, 58, 63, 65, 67, 70, 85
shimmer(s), 24, 41, 67, 70, 107
social media, 48
solitude, 38
spectrum/spectra, 6, 8, 18–20, 31, 74–75
spiritual borrowing, 1
spiritual direction, 4–5, 17, 42, 51, 53–54, 58
spiritual director, 4, 54, 65–66
step-by-step, vii, 23
success, 32, 36, 45, 51–52
Symeon, Saint, 86

Taoist, 85
Teresa of Avila, Saint, 88
therapist, 4, 54
transcendental meditation, 25
transiency, 10, 14–15, 17, 20

unpredictability, 16–17, 20

Varieties of Religious Experience, 9, 16–18, 90
vision(s), 19, 76, 82–83, 87–88, 90, 92, 94–95, 101, 104, 108
voice(s), 70–71, 81, 84–85, 87–88, 96–97, 103, 107

Wesley, John, 89
wind, 100, 104

www.ingramcontent.com/pod-product-compliance
Lightning Source LLC
Chambersburg PA
CBHW032232080426
42735CB00008B/823